Flourishing Life

Flourishing Life

Now and in the Time to Come

~

Sandra M. Levy-Achtemeier

CASCADE *Books* · Eugene, Oregon

FLOURISHING LIFE
Now and in the Time to Come

Cascade Books
An Imprint of Wipf and Stock Publishers
199 W. 8th Ave., Suite 3
Eugene, OR 97401

www.wipfandstock.com

ISBN 13: 978-1-61097-685-5

Cataloging-in-Publication data:

Levy, Sandra M.

    Flourishing life : now and in the time to come / Sandra M. Levy-Achtemeier.

    xvi + p. 23 cm.—Includes bibliographical references and index.

    ISBN 13: 978-1-61097-685-5

    1. Self-perception—Religious aspects—Christianity. 2. Happiness—Religious Aspects—Christianity. 3. Psychology—Religious Aspects—Christianity. 4. Christianity—Psychology.

BV4598.3.L45.2012

Manufactured in the USA.

This book is dedicated
to the memory of Leon, who would be very proud,
and to Bud, my loving husband, with thanksgiving.

For it is in action, in dance and in music, in the kinetic thrusting upward of arms and legs and the throwing up and back of the head, that great joy finds its highest expression.

—Kay Redfield Jamison

We do not lose the yearning for God. Inside us is the constant thumping hope that all this means something, that our lives are somehow lasting, that our years and loves are not hollow.

—Rabbi David Wolpe

O God . . . to your deep inspiration which commands me to be, I shall respond by taking great care never to stifle nor distort nor waste my power to love and to do. Next, to your all-embracing providence which shows me at each moment, by the day's events, the next step to take and the next rung to climb, I shall respond by my care never to miss an opportunity of rising towards the level of spirit.

—Pierre Teilhard de Chardin

Contents

Acknowledgments

DURING THE three years or so I spent writing this book, a number of colleagues have read drafts of all or parts of the work, sometimes in fact more than once. The final pages thus represent an amalgam of thoughts, critical comments, suggestions, and questions along the way. My friend, Anita, has read and encouraged this writing over the years. Jerome Berryman, creator of Godly Play, read an early draft of the Foreword overview, and at the local level, Howard Pugh—a friend and English literature scholar—applied his critical editing skills line-by-line to the manuscript as a whole. My friends Karen Schilling at Miami University and Joel Green at Fuller Theological Seminary brought their own expertise in psychology, neuroscience, and resurrection theology to bear on the penultimate manuscript draft, which benefitted enormously from their comments. My son Kevin read the entire finished manuscript and raised some critical thoughts for my consideration, and my other son Brian added his hearty support during the whole writing process. And of course, I want to thank the editorial staff at Cascade Books, especially K. C. Hanson, editor in chief, who believed in the worth of this work and brought the whole project to final completion.

But my most special thanks and gratitude I give to Catherine C. Wallace, literary friend and writer in Chicago, and to Paul Achtemeier, my husband. Cate has been encouraging and supportive of my writing for many years, and this particular book would be much the poorer without her careful reading—not only of the last draft, but of the first and everything in between along the way. And Paul ("Bud" to his friends) has critically read and reread this whole project, has listened to both my elation and worries over it in the meantime, and has generally offered his loving support and unwavering encouragement over the years. To both Cate and Bud I give my profound gratitude, which lies deeper than mere words can convey.

Introduction

M ANY YEARS ago as I was just beginning my career as an academic psychologist (first career, I might add!), I decided that it might be important—while studying the experience of aging and the effects of retirement—to actually sit down and talk to people about how they viewed their own lives at that point. This approach to my subject matter may not be surprising to you. But having been trained as a clinical psychologist in the same institution that had once been the home of B. F. Skinner, such an open-ended, interview-centered approach to the subject was rather unusual, to say the least.

All in all, I interviewed approximately seventy just-retired staff and faculty at two mid-western universities. I reinterviewed about forty of them two years later (to assess their adjustment over time). This was the richest, most rewarding project that I carried out in my entire academic career. What made it so rich was the subjective and experiential approach I took with each person I interviewed. I simply asked them three questions in serial order, with follow-up questions both to round out their description and to find out some things I was particularly interested in knowing (for example, their mood at the time of interview). The three questions were these: "How would you describe your present life—your life as it seems to you now?" Then, after summing up what I had just heard them say about their present situation, I followed the first question with the second: "Let's look at your past. How would

1

you describe your past life?" Then upon reflecting back the sense of what they had just told me about their past, I asked: "And now of course, what about your future? How would you describe your future as you see it?"

After each retiree finished describing their sense of what the future held for them—what they imagined their future would be like—I summed up for them all that they had told me. I quickly discovered that in reflecting back to them what I had just heard, I gave back to them a sense of their whole life as they now imagined it—both as it existed for them in memory, and was projected in expectancy for their future life. This whole exchange of telling and listening, and then this final summing up and giving back to these persons their imagined life as a whole, was a profound experience—especially for them, but also for me. I will never forget three of the people I met.

W. R. was a retired professor of musicology in the university's very distinguished School of Fine Arts. He was a concert pianist, a performing artist with great artistic talent. We met in his practice studio at the university, a space that he was allowed to still use for practice and for private tutoring of individual student pianists.

But now at age seventy, he was also free to do the one thing he had wanted to do all his life. In addition to a very full and successful career as a pianist and teacher, W. R. was—at long last—studying Greek! He had enthusiastically embraced the study of this classical language, and this had now become his life project. His imagined future was filled with hoped for mastery of that language, allowing him to read Greek tragedy as it was written in its original language.

And then there was G. B., a staff member in the Psychology Department and an electronics wizard who had run the apparatus shop for the department. When we talked, he had just retired. I remember driving out through the countryside to his comfortable bungalow tucked in the woods. As we sat at his kitchen table in the morning light, he described a life full of satisfaction and pride at what he had built with his creative mind and hands. His imagined future was filled with plans and projects—with new inventions that were already underway. His full and joy-filled life was undiminished by age and transition into retirement.

And then there was D. M., a professor of sociology who retired early from the pressure of academic productivity—the stress of publishing and grant writing and all the rest of the strain that goes along with academic life. We met in his living room, a cozy place whose walls were lined with full bookshelves and hung with abstract art. We faced each other in comfortable chairs placed on each side of a fireplace. And as he answered my three questions, his whole imagined world unfolded as he told his life story.

D. M. had recently shocked his colleagues by retiring at age fifty-five to become, as he put it, a "consumer" rather than "producer" of cultural goods. He had been a productive academic with a stellar publishing record. But he had now turned his back on all that to "consume" with his wife all the good things they could enjoy together while they still had their health. They were going to spend winters in Florida rather than fight the Midwestern snows. They were going to travel, see plays, read what they wanted, go to art shows. And as D. M. talked gratefully about the luxury of cultural consumption, I—who was at the beginning of my "publish or perish" academic career—almost envied his retired life, seeing myself there already in his exuberantly imagined world as it lay before my mind's eye.

To anticipate a bit where we will travel in the pages ahead, these three—differing in educational background and personal values—nevertheless expressed gratitude, hope, and yes, even joy in their everyday lives. They had lived their lives to their creative fullness, and they were still growing, evolving, and transforming themselves in the process. In short, they were flourishing, despite whatever blows life had inevitably dealt them along the way.

I remember wondering even back then if there was some way that I might live my life so that in the end I could conclude—like W. R., G. B., and D. M. seemed to do—that it had all been a very good run. My hope was that as my energy and days dwindled, I could look back and see that I had lived my life to the fullest—instead of fidgeting it away, scrambling through life's maze without deep purpose or coherent meaning.

Aristotle viewed the elderly as the only ones who could look back and appraise whether they had lived a good life or not. And my listening deeply for hours to stories told by these seventy or so aged persons, was not only a moving experience, but one imparting wisdom as well. And these three particular life stories, the life narratives told by W. R., D. M., and G. B., stand out because in hindsight I viewed them as not only models of successful life transition, but also as models of an overall life well lived. There was a sense of meaningful continuity to their stories, an integrity, an integration of disposition and talent, context and culture, that gave their lives a certain authentic coherence. Despite the fact that two of them were past sixty-five and the other in his mid-fifties, each was an exemplar of life still flourishing into middle and old age.

Unfortunately, not all those to whom I listened were such exemplars. Some retirees were bitter, some depressed, some still fixed and clinging desperately to a role they no longer had in a field that had let them go into the oblivion of a forced retirement. Joshua Shenk, the author of a recent article in the *Atlantic*, found the same amazing variability in life flourishing in a study of Harvard undergraduates who he followed for some seventy-two years. He observes that "mature adaptations are a real-life alchemy, a way of turning the dross of emotional crises, pain . . . into the gold of human connection, accomplishment, and creativity."[1] But in that Harvard study, just as with some of my interviewees, not all the alchemy turned dross into gold. Many who began with talent and vigor ended their lives in failure.

So the questions to be addressed in this present book are these. How can we live now so that our lives over time achieve the coherence and the happiness displayed in these three lives given

1. Shenk, "Want Makes Us Happy?" 44.

here? W. R., G. B., and D. M. had each lived fully engaged and creative lives for many decades. What were the roots of that flourishing? Are there behaviors that can be changed, practices that can be carried out prior to old age, that enhance such flourishing—even in the face of trauma, loss, or sickness? As a psychologist, therapist, and pastor I have seen individuals show incredible resilience and positive transformation even despite—or perhaps because of—trauma happening to them in their lives. What is the wellspring of such human resilience?

I'll draw from multiple fields of inquiry to provide some pretty clear answers to the questions of why some flourish and how such flourishing can be enhanced: Evolutionary neuroscience and its philosophical underpinnings; what is currently termed "positive psychology"; and some aspects of contemporary theology. Blending all three fields together, the vision of human being that emerges is an embodied or incarnate soul, essentially relational in nature. Created in the image of our Creator God, we are endowed neurologically with the power to transcend our selves and engage with others, as well as encounter the Other who created us all.

Let's take a look ahead. In prologue 1, I introduce the notion of a coherent life. In Chapter 1, "The Embodied Self and the Flourishing Life," we'll consider the meaning of being human, from genes to culture. In chapter 2, "Embodied Practices and the Flourishing Life," we'll look at individual spiritual practices—from ritual to storytelling—at the intersection of community and culture.

Prologue 2 introduces the next chapter and sketches out three biographies of individuals I consider exemplars of flourishing, despite great personal loss and trauma. In chapter 3, "Creating a Flourishing Life through Suffering and Loss," we'll look at what these three stories have in common. In the process, we'll see how the good story which gives overall meaning to their lives leads to satisfaction, as well as to a coherent sense of integrity and an overall sense of life well lived.

Finally, in chapter 4, "The Ultimate Flourishing: Resurrected Life and Kingdom Living," we will examine the biblical and theological bases for belief in a bodily resurrection. I conclude this book by considering our own resurrection beyond personal death because a flourishing that results only in psychological and social betterment is, in my view, still sorely limited. Thus, we'll develop a vision of final flourishing consistent with the view of human nature developed over the course of this work. As many others have noted, as long as we humans are subject to death, we cannot be fundamentally free to flourish in any final way.

I contend that we are embodied souls, purposely engaged in a world of meaning. Our lives can be enriched and we can indeed flourish by building on human strengths through various practices that have been shown to enhance a flourishing life across the adult years. Our whole, embodied selves, through our powers of imagination, reflection and self-transcendence, are open to God's impingement, inspiration, and revelation in our everyday lives. We are indeed spirited bodies, through and through. And our ultimate flourishing will be as embodied selves before the face of God (metaphorically speaking!). Whether you are a doubtful seeker after truth and deep meaning in your life, or whether you are a devout believer in God, this book should inform your journey.

Prologue 1

The Coherent Life and Human Flourishing

Evolution and the Human Journey toward Transcendence

IMAGINE YOU were asked to engage in a ritual of some kind that made no sense to you, that was foreign to your experience. Maybe you wound up at some motivational conference or in some California retreat setting for body/mind healing, or some such. And you were asked to stand in a circle, holding hands and chanting some sacred sound or maybe passing an orange around the circle without using your hands. Maybe you took part in some Native American ritual and found yourself sitting in a sweat lodge in order to purify your body. Or maybe you were not raised in any kind of religious tradition, but you got talked into attending an Easter Vigil service at the local Episcopal church and you stood around outside gazing at the lighting of the Easter fire and then filed into the church, clutching a little candle in your sweaty right hand.

And what maybe did you feel? Silly? Self-conscious? Physically awkward?

It seems that you just can't will yourself into a ritual in any meaningful way if you are not steeped in the tradition, if you are not part of a culture that has in part shaped your body and mind—your embodied, meaning-making brain—both your unconscious and conscious sense of what feels right to your person. Actions become meaningful through a process of *coherence*. Such coherence extends from your body and its sense-making brain to your culture, which in part supplies the brain's "meaning menu," and gives guidance regarding values and purposes in life. Of course, you were born into a particular culture willy-nilly. But you can also choose your cultural context and embrace a new one along the way, being reshaped in the process. That is, it's possible to transform your life as an adult by moving from a less-than-optimal or even a tension-filled life to one of greater coherence across all levels of your experience.

For instance, I was raised in a moderately religious home, a Christian one where we went to a Protestant church on Sundays and observed the high holy days of Easter and Christmas with special celebrations. But as an adolescent (as very typical for that stage of life) I began to reflect on life's meaning and create my own identity as a person distinct from my parents' definition of myself. And since the culture I was part of was unquestionably a religious one, I turned to religion as I pieced together my self story. By the time I was a high school senior, I converted to Catholicism because I found the rituals, the symbols, the liturgies compelling and attractive.

I attended a Catholic college and decided at one point to enter a religious order and become a nun. But somewhere along the way, that plan became derailed and I got married instead, had two wonderful little boys, and went on to graduate school, earning a PhD in psychology.

To make a long story short, by a series of all those decisions that we make that wind up shaping our lives and our futures, I wound up at a major university, aggressively building an academic career—publishing or perishing—and I was pretty good at the game. I happened to land in an area of research that was just taking off, I had wonderful collaborators, and my academic career moved into high orbit. I published a fair amount, jetted around the world giving papers, received grants from some pretty prestigious places, and wound up on various boards and executive committees that filled out my curriculum vitae.

But all through this academic period, I was nagged by the sense that none of it really meant much to me. I would ask colleagues at parties what they would do if they found out they had only two years to live. And I was amazed that many of them said they would continue in just what they were doing. I knew I wouldn't. I'd be out of there like a shot.

Finally, one weekend I went off to a religious retreat setting to think about the direction of my life. I projected myself ahead to age eighty and imagined looking back over my lifetime. From that vantage point I tried to view what I might wish that I had done with my life in the meantime. It became clear to me that the story I had written so far was not an authentic one, my current projects and goals were not consistent—not coherent—with my deepest sense of felt worth and meaning. The cultural context I had immersed myself within was actually detrimental to my character, to the deepest values and virtues I aspired to in my life.

At that point—and with the encouragement of my husband, by the way—I turned explicitly to the traditional context of the church. Over some months of reflection, and with the great support of friends and clergy and family, I decided to leave academia and attend seminary to study for the Episcopal priesthood. And during those months after the decision was made, but before I made my announcement to the academic community, I knew nothing but great joy and peace. After my decision was made widely known, colleagues wondered aloud whether it was painful for me to give up now all that I had worked for in my academic career over the past fourteen years. But I never knew a minute of pain! Only the joy of being true to my own needs and values, and the comfort and welcome of a tradition and community that embraced me in the process.

I had rewritten my story. And in that process I had achieved for the first time in years a coherent life structure, a sense of coherent wholeness. This wholeness encompassed both my embodied, implicit sense of life's meaning and the cultural context within which I created my new story with a new future. In the rewriting, I gave my life a sense of coherent meaning that it had lacked for so many years.

Interestingly, I have also discovered that the very writing of this book—pulling together and integrating my first field of academic psychology and my current life of pastoral and theological concerns—has further created coherence in my life at this point. I have also found that underneath it all, God is somehow in the midst of all this business of being fully human and living a flourishing life.

So in a nutshell, this is my story. But I give it only to illustrate what I mean by coherence and the role of personal story or narrative as the glue that holds the meaning together, from body to culture. I have drawn, of course, an oversimplified picture to merely introduce some sense of what I mean by moving from incoherence to coherence as part of life's ongoing, meaning-making venture. Further, let me state the obvious: your story, wherever you are in life's trek, will undoubtedly look and feel quite different. No two stories are alike. But there are some things I can say about us in general, some things I can say here about the nature of being human, about what we all share, and about what might go into making a life well lived.

Both evolutionary neuroscience and positive psychology refer to "upward" patterns in human development—a movement toward greater complexity, a directional pull toward self-transcendence, a developmental move toward what is perceived as good. Findings within these two scientific fields are consistent with what theology describes as God's pull toward greater human excellence or flourishing.

From the field of *evolutionary neuroscience*: "Humans are . . . unique in ways that defy [reductionistic] evolutionary explanation and point to our spiritual nature. This includes the existence of the Moral law (the knowledge of right and wrong) and the search for God that characterizes all human cultures throughout history."[1] "There is a trend in human evolution toward spiritualization of consciousness."[2]

From the field of *psychology*: "Although the human organism certainly has the power to 'go bad' if life contexts push it that way, people are otherwise directed toward growth, connection, and integration . . . [Researchers] have now amassed considerable evidence supporting the idea of a positive, health-relevant bias within human nature, which leads people to move toward greater self-concordance and more intrinsic valuing over time."[3] In short, humans tend to evolve toward more coherence as they age.

From the field of *theology*: "It is impossible to justify evolution toward increasing complexity . . . without imagining that somewhere, making itself felt in the very heart of evolution, there is a centre that is sufficiently independent and active to force . . . the whole of the cosmos to . . . itself in the likeness of that centre."[4]

In this last quotation, Pierre Teilhard de Chardin is referring to what he calls the Omega point, drawing all creation to itself, the Omega otherwise known in his theology as God. This ultimate theme in Teilhard's writings has been echoed in the writings of other, more contemporary theologians whom we will turn to in

1. Collins, *The Language of God*, 200.

2. Beauregard and O'Leary, *The Spiritual Brain*, 295.

3. Sheldon, *Optimal Human Being*, 138.

4. Teilhard de Chardin, *Let Me Explain*, 84 (quotation from *The Phenomenon of Man*).

later chapters. Teilhard's evolutionary theology and his understanding of the meaning of being human in its deepest sense have been very influential in both literary as well as theological circles.

Summarizing the theological point, there is an ultimate Cause, a transcendent Other, who is actively engaged with the world about us. I believe that God's Spirit penetrates, enlivens, and sustains all of creation. Creation itself is being drawn toward a final destination, whether we want to refer to this endpoint as the kingdom of God, or the Omega Point of Christ's Being, or the fullness of a transformed creation on earth or the eschaton. We are all at least potentially receivers of God's grace-filled Spirit and we are all equipped with embodied minds or souls to respond to God's impingement in our lives.

But unfortunately, our stories can go bad. Our marvelous creative power can turn toward evil. We can shut off the Divine call, and we can as individuals and as a society literally destroy ourselves. Yet it is also possible for us to pay attention to our best inclinations, to open our minds to God's impingement by engaging in various practices within contexts that promote human flourishing. It is possible to evolve joyfully into more flourishing, coherent selves. It is possible to create and embrace a life well lived in the stories we make and remake of our lives, contributing to the story of humankind on an ascending course.

Let us turn now and begin this present journey together.

1

The Embodied Self and the Flourishing Life

A GREAT DEAL has been written in recent years concerning the evolution of the human mind over the millennia, and the emergence of culture and conscience as humans developed the capacity for symbol making and language. Like our species, cultures evolved as humans created tools for writing and passing on their thoughts to unseen others in the wider community. Today, psychologists and neuroscientists understand the human brain as a map of that evolutionary development.

The evolutionary base to human development and the biological ground for what is termed the "emergent mind" have become widely accepted even at the popular level. At the same time, the question of the soul and the place of God or a divine Creator in this scientific scenario has been raised in many quarters. And of course the opposing camps have become strident in their rhetoric.

There is the antitheistic camp, represented by Christopher Hitchens's bestseller, *God is not Great*, and their nihilistic argument that we are nothing but meat, and when the body dies, that's it. There are the Creationists at the other extreme, arguing the case for taking the Bible literally. And there are those in the middle, who accept the overwhelming evidence for human evolutionary

13

development, but insist on an Intelligent Designer who alone could have planned such complex human creatures. Recently, a more nuanced integration of belief in God's creative purpose in evolutionary design and the scientific understanding of evolutionary development has been offered by proponents of "evolutionary theism." This version lies closest to my own views of the matter.

Probably the most prominent proponent of this latter view is Francis Collins, the head of the Human Genome Project and now head of the National Institutes of Health. In his book *The Language of God*,[1] Collins says the following: "God, who is not limited in space or time, created the universe and established natural laws that govern it. Seeking to populate this otherwise sterile universe with living creatures, God chose the elegant mechanism of evolution to create microbes, plants and animals of all sorts. Most remarkably, God intentionally chose the same mechanism to give rise to special creatures who would have intelligence, a knowledge of right and wrong, free will, and a desire to seek fellowship with Him."[2]

Many evolutionary neuroscientists today admit that human consciousness and the capacity for self-reflection finally cannot be reduced to neural firings in the brain. The emergence of the sense of self and the self's awareness of itself are finally seen as a "miracle," unexplainable in biological terms. Collins and others such as Nancey Murphy and Mario Beauregard are explicit about their faith-based approaches to God and evolution, recognizing where science leaves off and Mystery begins. "The theistic evolution perspective cannot, of course, prove that God is real, as no logical argument can fully achieve that. Belief in God will always require a leap of faith."[3]

Here is my main point. As Collins and others have stressed, science was never intended to answer, nor *can* it answer, questions

1. Collins, *The Language of God*.

2. Ibid., 200–201.

3. Ibid., 201.

of why the universe exists at all, or questions about the deepest meaning of human life. What ultimately will become of humanity? What will happen to each one of us after death? Belief in a Transcendent Other always lies outside scientific discourse. The experience of God's revelation in Scripture, in prayer, in ritual, and in our everyday lives is ultimately a matter of faithful openness and receptivity to such encounters with the divine.

But nothing in the findings of evolutionary science contradicts such a belief in God's reality. And thus for Collins and for many others, we need not choose between science and faith, but can view the two domains of discourse as complementary and mutually enriching.

~

What does it mean to live a coherent life, to flourish as fully as possible in the time we are allotted?

There does seem to be—not only for our species but for individuals as well—an innate tendency toward spiritual growth over our lifetime. There is empirical evidence that as individuals age, they tend to report greater life satisfaction, a greater sense of well-being and joy in living, less anxiety and conflict in their lives, a greater sense of altruism and satisfaction with their lives as a whole. Kennon Sheldon puts it this way: "humans [can be seen] as self-organizing, dynamical systems that contain a nature and built-in impetus for positive development and change . . . Humans are inherently growth oriented and pro-socially oriented, until adaptation to problematic circumstance forestalls or forestays these impulses [toward the good]."[4] In general, Sheldon concludes that if the environment is reasonably supportive, people tend to veer toward enhanced well-being over time.

George Valliant, a Harvard psychiatrist who has studied the lives of graduates from that institution for decades, concludes in his work *Spiritual Evolution* that the human brain is hard-wired to

4. Sheldon, *Optimal Human Being,* 67.

generate positive emotions (love, joy, peace, forgiveness, hope, and so on). The neural connections binding these emotional centers to areas of the brain concerned with memory and moral reasoning grow over time as we age.

Starting in adolescence, such brain connections are pruned and strengthened. Such growth is reflected in social connections and commitments both to others and to a greater purpose beyond our own individual concerns. In fact, Valliant defines human spirituality itself as this coupling of positive emotions (such as love) with self-transcendence—with reaching out to others in communal bonding. While recognizing differences between individuals in the final intensity of such "spiritual illumination," nevertheless Valliant insists that all humans are spiritual to some extent. All have the potential to grow spiritually over the course of their entire lives because the neural connections involved continue to grow to age sixty and perhaps beyond.

I should mark here one caution. N. T. Wright and others criticize much of the biologically based, evolutionary picture of human flourishing as a mere "parody of Christian vision." A simplistic espousing of the notion that "every day in every way we are getting better and better," cannot finally account for or deal with evil. Obviously evil abounds, both within ourselves as sometimes greedy and selfish persons, as well as within institutions and communities. So as we shall see over the course of these pages, our *potential* for flourishing is not always realized. Outer circumstance and inner frailty can stifle individual growth. Poor personal stories can be patched together reflecting despair and leading to life's dead ends. Horrendous evil—caused by humans or not—can overwhelm us. In the end, the selves we create through our life story can remain static and disjointed—and so a life ends as a mere shadow of what it might have become.

But within the theistic and incarnational or embodied framework that I am building here, flourishing is always possible—no matter what life's vicissitudes, no matter what happens to us in life.

God calls each of us to create a life story that gives meaning and invigorates our future growth. And God has endowed each of us with the capacity to self-transcend, to find God in all things, to commit ourselves to others and to God's good purpose.

But what is the shape of a life well lived? Perhaps the simplest answer is by making the most out of what you are born with (inborn traits) and what you are given by the people and the culture around you (adaptations, goals, and stories).

BRAINS AND TRAITS
(OR, HOW YOU ARE LIKE EVERYONE ELSE)

In Jonathan Haidt's work *The Happiness Hypothesis*,[5] he develops a very useful metaphor to describe human functioning. Haidt uses the metaphor of *elephant* to describe our genetically based, embodied consciousness as we have evolved as human beings over time. This level of brain function involves autonomic processes that maintain life, as well as sensory, perceptual, and motor activities and trait characteristics that are gene driven and largely out of our direct control. Haidt employs the metaphor *rider* to describe our rational, "higher consciousness" situated in the neocortex—the latest "brain" to develop in our evolutionary history.

As Haidt describes it, these two metaphorical creatures have evolved their own kind of essential human wisdom, and they also interact with one another. The rider—our evolved, higher consciousness—allows us to use language, to make moral judgments, to reason, to plan, to delay gratification, and to make decisions in our everyday life. It also gives us the ability to create our life's overall meaning by the stories we weave. The elephant—situated in the lower regions of the brain—is the source of our desires and our emotion-based sensing, our embodied knowing of our world in which we move and have a self.

---

5. Haidt, *The Happiness Hypothesis*, 2006.

The dynamic interplay between elephant and rider reflects a holistic, embodied way of being a whole self. That is, the elephant and its rider are neurologically and functionally intertwined and integrated across all levels of human experience. If I am anxious about being fired as I approach my boss's office door, my heart rate speeds up and my palms sweat in the face of possible threat. If I'm embarrassed at a social or moral gaff, I blush. If I decide to practice daily prayer meditation or work in a food bank, neural connections supporting positive emotions and moral reasoning are strengthened.

Haidt says, "when the neocortex came along, it made the rider possible, but it made the elephant much smarter too."[6] Exercising power through language and reason, our newest level of brain matter has only limited ability to run the entire show. The elephant—that seat of our emotionally based knowledge of our world, our inherited traits and personality dispositions—knows what it knows, and wants what it wants. And as much as the rider works to tame the elephant's desires, ultimately, the elephant goes where it wants. Our vast reservoir of embodied knowledge, needs, wants, and dispositional tendencies moves us forward in life.

It takes a great deal of patience, time, and practice to tame the elephant. If the rider attempts to order the elephant around against its will, conflicts between reason and emotion erupt. Nine times in ten, the emotions win out. (Think of the last time you warned yourself against an emotional course of action, say falling in love with the wrong person or taking that second piece of chocolate cake or glass of good Cabernet. Who won?) But there are ways to tame the elephant, and we'll consider some of them in a later chapter. For now, lets linger with the elephant for a while and briefly consider universal human traits. In other words, let's think about how you and I are, in one way or the other, pretty much like everyone else in the world.

6. Ibid., 13. The neocortex is the most recently developed part of the brain, that region of the cerebral cortex unique to mammals.

I have three friends with whom I have lunch every month or so. We joke that all together we make a complete, ideal person. Focusing only on the most dominant characteristics, Anne is generous, goodhearted, and sensitive to the opinions of others; Becky is caring and warm and outgoing; Anita is vivacious, open, and welcoming—hospitable to all. And then there is me: cerebral and somewhat introverted and reserved. Yep, the four of us altogether a complete, well-rounded human being!

Of course, Anne, Anita, and Becky and I are much more complex persons than my cursory, surface sketch above suggests. If you asked my husband or closest friend, they might say, "Well, she has a tendency to be introverted . . . likes small dinner parties with close friends rather than big cocktail parties . . . likes to go off to a cabin in the woods by herself once in a while . . . and so on. But really . . . put her in front of a large audience . . . or at the coffee hour of her parish . . . and you'll see her light up, 'work the room,' and love doing it!"

No, we're all more complex than our basic dispositional tendencies would suggest. *Who* we are has more to do with our goals and values. It has more to do with the communities we embrace, and these communities in turn help shape our activities and our life stories over time. But focusing on these biologically based characteristic tendencies, such largely inherited traits provide others with clues to our actions within a group setting.

Think about the guy you got stuck with the last time you were placed next to a stranger at a dinner party—that loudmouth who went on and on stereotyping the newly elected black mayor, monopolizing the conversation the whole time. Even without the technical language, you might have immediately "diagnosed" him as an extrovert, along with seeing him as close-minded and bigoted, as well as an overall disagreeable person.

And it turns out that on an intuitive level, you would have recognized three of the five universally evolved human traits pretty much found across all cultures worldwide. These five universal traits—extroversion (versus introversion), neuroticism (versus even-keeled and non-anxiousness), conscientiousness (versus irresponsibility), agreeableness (versus disagreeableness and social rudeness), and openness to experience (versus rigidity and close-mindedness)—are genetically based. But their *expression* is shaped by context and community.

That is, along with genes, our own developmental history has a shaping effect on trait tendencies and their expression. So our disposition to think, feel, and act in a certain way is based on both our biological constitution and our personal developmental history.[7] Our evolved, genetic design is merely a blueprint. It is not a fixed and completely determined program—or as they say, genes are not destiny. This dispositional signature each of us possesses appears to be the most easily recognizable and stable aspect of each one of us as social selves.

Although we can quickly size up a stranger using these five categorical types, the trait cluster itself doesn't predict actual day-to-day behavior very well. The fact that I'm somewhat introverted will not necessarily predict my social behavior on any given day in any given situation. Recognizing a dinner partner as a rigid bigot provides only limited predictability in terms of any particular behavior of his at any particular time.

Let's say, for example, that his beloved only daughter brings home a college classmate who is black. She has fallen in love with him and has already decided to marry. (You could stretch the example and imagine that the classmate is female!) Based on just your initial impression of your dinner partner, you might guess he'd go ballistic at the prospect. But then you might be surprised. Because maybe it turns out that based on the strength of his family and religious values, his ingrained sense of hospitality and sense of himself as a fair person, as well as on the love he bears for his daughter, he warmly welcomes the classmate into his family circle.

7. Kennon, *Optimal Human Being*, 2004.

So while it may be that first impressions count, they aren't particularly accurate in predicting actual behavior.

No, in order to go beyond grasping *what kind* of person the dinner partner is, in order to know *who* he is, we have to look in a more fine-grained way at his goals, his motivations and values, and the social roles he has chosen. We have to dig a little deeper into his own individual development within the family, community, and perhaps religious contexts that have shaped him and that he has continued to embrace—into how he as rider has trained his elephant. So let's turn for a brief look at the level of individual adaptations, or how you and I are like *some* other people.[8]

ADAPTATIONS AND GOALS
(OR, HOW YOU ARE LIKE SOME OTHER PEOPLE)

I want to frame this discussion in the widest way possible. So let's step back and consider again some of the ideas developed by Pierre Teilhard de Charidin, whom we referred to at the beginning of this chapter. In his *The Divine Milieu*, Teilhard sees our lives from two angles: "Each . . . existence [is] divided into two parts—what [one] does and what [one] undergoes." At times we are active; at other times we are acted upon and are passive. And in each life "we shall find at the outset that, in accordance with his promise, God truly waits for us in things, unless indeed he advances to meet us."[9] God calls and engages us in our life's creative choices, and accomplishments and God meets us in the midst of our passivities or losses of this life, including finally sickness and death.

As we have seen, each of us is born with a genetic blueprint that includes our disposition to act and react in signature or

8. Referring to our elephant and rider metaphor, we might see this as the level of interaction between the two creatures. While the elephant is motivated to pursue self-serving ends, the rider can shape the motivational direction by paying attention to community constraints and opportunities, and by taming the elephant (to a certain extent) through various practices.

9. Teilhard de Chardin, *The Divine Milieu*, 47.

characteristic ways in social groups. But we are born into cultures and communities that have a profound influence—not only on the expression of these dispositional traits, but also on our values and social roles and goals that we pursue as active agents in our own lives. The world around us will impinge willy-nilly, enhancing or impeding our individual development, enhancing our embodied spiritual selves or (as Teilhard puts it) "poisoning" us.

It is the basic premise here that God is active in our daily lives, calling to us and penetrating the world about us. Teilhard says "God, in all that is most loving and incarnate in him, is not far away from us . . . Rather he awaits us every instant in our action, in the work of the moment. There is a sense in which [God] is at the tip of my pen, my spade, my brush, my needle—of my heart and of my thought."[10] In openness to God's presence and in collaboration with God's call in our everyday lives, we are lured into fashioning our own self through our commitments and our projects.

According to Teilhard's thinking, you and I are called to cooperate in fashioning our own embodied souls. Starting with what we inherit from all who have gone before us (the "natural territory of the self"), we are to build a work, "an opus," as a particular part of an infinite Opus that surrounds, yet transcends us. Creation continues and we serve to complete it through our own life projects. In this view, nothing is profane, but the whole world is God drenched—in short, a divine milieu in which we play our part through all our earthly days, growing and developing over the days we are given.

But our lives are also made up of the things that happen to us, that befall us, that thwart our plans and projects, that ultimately bring us down in sickness and death. Teilhard says, "we undergo life as much as we undergo death, if not more."[11] But there is also a way to embrace such limits and losses, to grow and to be transformed in the process. We can overcome some blocks by finding

10. Ibid., 64.
11. Ibid., 76.

another way to accomplish plans, to overcome the odds and come out the other side even stronger and better. And in the end, when there's no way around the loss, we can bear the limits beyond our control, meeting God within what befalls us and freely embracing the grace of God as he perfects his creation in us. That open invitation is there, and our potential for responding to it is built into our embodied selves. Whether we accept the invitation or not is the question to be answered by each one of us as we walk the earth for a short space of our given time.

Let's focus a bit on these adaptations each of us makes in response to the world we meet. That elephant and its rider live out their lives in the midst of a herd. As Haidt puts it, "Seneca was right: 'No one can live happily who has regard to himself alone and transforms everything into a question of his own utility.' John Donne was right: No man, woman, or child is an island. Aristophanes was right: We need others to complete us. *We are an ultrasocial species*, full of emotions finely tuned for loving, befriending, helping, sharing, and otherwise intertwining our lives with others."[12] And again ultimately, we are open to God's Spirit calling in our lives.

It is at this level of goals, values, roles, and adaptations that change is most likely to occur through various practices and community reinforcement. Think about your own life course and how likely it is that some of your values and goals have changed over time. In my own life, I shifted my plans, goals, and social role from academic striver to seminarian and to the life of a clergy person, creating a profound shift in my self-image and identity over a period of a year or so of transition. And the communities I embraced, in turn, shaped me. The academic community I was part of for so many years was very clear about what was valued and what was not, what would get you tenure and what would count for little. And so it turns out was—and is—the Church as an institution and culture.

12. Haidt, *The Happiness Hypothesis*, 133–34, italics added.

Contexts and practices matter, from the neural connections in our brains to the stories we tell that give meaning to our lives. In the chapters ahead, we'll return to this discussion as we consider religious communities as creators of coherence in our life stories.

STORIES AND CULTURE
(OR, HOW YOU ARE LIKE NOBODY ELSE)

Elie Wiesel, writer and Holocaust survivor, once said that "God made man because He loves stories." And since we are made in God's image, we love stories, too. In fact, we humans are wired to think in story form, and from our earliest childhood (around age three), we weave together sequences of events to capture and explain to ourselves what happens and what will happen in the world about us.

And in that telling, we create our identity as actors in the world, providing some sense of continuity from past to present and to what may come. Donald Polkinghorne gives one of the best descriptions of this self-making through narration. "We achieve our personal identities and self-concept through the use of the narrative . . . and make our existence into a whole by understanding it as an expression of a single unfolding and developing story. We are in the middle of our stories and cannot be sure how they will end; we are constantly having to revise the plot as new events are added to our lives. Self, then, is not a static thing or a substance, but a configuring of personal events into an historical unity that includes not only what one has been but also anticipations of what one will be."[13]

So we tell our stories and in the process, we tell the *meaning* of ourselves into being. But what then is a story? From our earliest childhood we have listened to the stories read to us by our parents or parent surrogates. I couldn't wait to hear my dad's nightly story of Beezlebum, an imaginary character who did marvelous feats!

13. Polkinghorne, *Narrative Knowing and the Human Sciences*, 150.

We have told stories of our own to our children and to our friends, and so we have a deep grasp of what a story is like. We know one when we hear one.

But some have tried to refine our understanding of what makes a story a story, and so let's take a closer look. In his *Acts of Meaning*, Jerome Bruner identifies five properties of stories to help us flesh out the concept.[14] First, stories have plots. That is, there is a certain sequence to the telling, a "first this and then that." Stories have a certain implied time course embedded in them.

Second, stories can be real or fictional, and sometimes it's quite hard to draw the line between the two—there's a certain blurring between fiction and reality. We tell the story of what happened to us that was embarrassing last week, and we embellish the telling with metaphors that expand the concrete meaning beyond the mere facts. "I was mortified when she said that to me, I was bowled over, I was blown away!" Now the hearer understands that I was not literally knocked off my feet, and the telling of the concrete facts becomes expanded beyond the objective event into a realm of metaphoric meaning. The story I told has then a power beyond the concrete and thus a "factual indifference," to use Bruner's phrase.

The third property of story according to Bruner is its functional use in giving meaning to the unexpected, to events that disrupt cultural expectation, or acceptable cultural patterns.

Normally we don't tell stories that are prosaic, banal, and boring repetitions about our everyday occurrences. Just because I went to the grocery store yesterday, this is not an interesting tale to tell. Only if when I pulled into the parking lot, some woman made an obscene gesture to me as I pulled into the last parking space does such a breach of the expected everyday background become worthy of a story when I return home to relay it.

In fact, Bruner makes much of this particular functional aspect of storytelling. We explain, we justify, we give moral meaning to, and we negotiate meaning when the unusual occurs,

14. Bruner, *Acts of Meaning*, 43–52.

maintaining the social equilibrium by the stories we tell. Thus, the unusual is made somehow to take its place (or become coherent) within the norm by the meaning we give to explain our lives. And this self-justification through story begins at a very early age. But more about that shortly.

Fourth, stories have a certain dramatic quality, heightened by the use of figures of speech, rhetorical devices such as metaphors and analogies, colorful symbolic expressions that give both ambiguity and drama, catching our attention and fascinating us in the telling. Every good preacher knows the importance of stories to make a point that won't be forgotten. (And the stories themselves won't be forgotten! So you might recycle sermons, but you can't recycle the stories embedded in them!)

Finally, stories have what Bruner calls a "dual landscape."[15] That is, if our stories ring true there is a link between the meaning we create in them and our behaviors in our social world. This holds for the episodic stories we create to explain everyday events (like the parking lot episode), as well as the story of our life as a whole—whether fully expressed or not. So in general, let's put it this way. Your actions are authentic and ring true (or are coherent) if they reflect the meaning you give to your life. And you weave together this meaning of yourself out of memories of your past and expectations for your future as it's likely to unfold over time.

Developmentally, we are born into a world that is a cultural given, a world first composed of primary family, that "vicar of culture," as Bruner puts it. The key parent, usually the mother, coos and talks to the child, the parents fill the child with family stories, and the child overhears the stories that the resident adults tell to one another. So over the months and early years the young child develops and assumes a sense of his or her world, its ways and means, its values and beliefs, and how things are supposed to be done in order to fit that world's expectations.

15. Ibid., 51–52.

By around the age of three, an "extended self" has emerged, a self capable of remembering the past and reflecting on its meaning and a self capable of envisioning alternative futures. In his book *How Our Lives Become Stories*, Paul Eakin says it is this extended self, this temporal self, that is the foundation for autobiography, providing a prenarrative structure in our consciousness that "supports and sustains our . . . sense of who we are."[16] But this extended self of memory and anticipation emerges out of and is built upon our earlier grasp of our social world and how it works and where we fit within it—developed long before we had any language to put it altogether. Once we have the language, we explain ourselves and others' actions through the stories we tell, and we create a sense of ongoing self in the process. Thus, the self identity is constructed jointly by both child and family. But at some point the child outgrows the family's vicarage, and larger institutions—school and church or synagogue—carry the culture's meaning.

As we saw in Polkinghorne's definition I quoted at the beginning of this section, this telling of ourselves extends across a lifetime. And in those stories, we give an account of ourselves, incorporating our goals and social accommodations that we make along the way. And if the story is a good one, we achieve some kind of coherent sense of self as we tell our lives. Whether we are telling "stories from the crib" or piecing together our life meaning in adolescence or later adulthood, we are engaged essentially in the same meaning-making process. We elaborate the events in our lives that stand out, the turning points, the traumas, the embarrassing episodes, the joys and surprises, giving them meaning within a community. We tie them together in the largest picture we can, still writing our stories to the end.

Adolescence—that time of often intense, romantic idealism—appears to be a peak period for our first putting together our own philosophy of life, of struggling to make sense out of where we have been and where we are going. It was around the age of

16. Eakin, *How Our Lives Become Stories*, 102.

fifteen that I had a life-changing conversion to Roman Catholicism and embraced a whole theology of life, rewriting my self-identity in the process.

Coincident with this adolescent "myth-making" ("a patterned integration of our remembered past, perceived present, and anticipated future")[17] is the development of certain brain structures providing the neurological structure for such story making. For it is during the period of late adolescence and early adulthood that certain brain pathways are pruned and others are strengthened, linking more firmly the brain's memory and positive emotion centers with the neural centers providing the base for moral reasoning. We become biologically equipped to lay out the meaning of our lives to ourselves and to others.

The cultural world that surrounds us and in which we are embedded from adolescence onward profoundly influences our life stories. And it turns out that there are characteristic or typical stories that get told within particular cultural contexts. Americans typically tell stories of independent triumph (Horatio Alger themes), of overcoming odds through individual hard work, of competitive striving and competing and winning, and so on.

But at the individual level, beneath and beside the typical, are our individual stories shaped by those around us and with whom we have conversations that matter. You and I live in a network of others who co-create our stories out of the dialogues in which we engage. We also express our meaning in our practices, which in turn, create meaning in our lives. We achieve a unified sense of self out of our ongoing story, revising and editing as we go along through our days.

As Bruner puts it, "culture provides guides and strategies for finding a niche between stability and change. It exhorts, forbids, lures, constrains, and rewards. And the self, with the capacity for reflection and imagination escapes or embraces or reevaluates or

17. McAdams, *The Stories We Live By*, 12.

reformulates what culture has to offer." The self selects from culture's menu and tells a story like no one else's.

~

Allow me to dip into my own autobiographical journey once more. I began this section of the book by describing my identity transformation when I rewrote my life story, shifting from academic self with associated goals and values to clergy self, with a whole different plot frame carrying my life story along. On reflection, I think what I achieved in that rewriting was a greater *vertical* coherence between life-long religious values imprinted during adolescence (that's another story!)—the embodied elephant's assumed world of background meaning—and renewed goals, values, and practices within my new narrative framework—assembled by the rider.

But some years before that transforming rewriting, I had faced another turning point in my life that required a shift in self-identity. For a number of years I had been Chief of the Behavioral Medicine Branch at the National Cancer Institute. And in that role, with the knowledge and approval of my director, I had carried out my own research project and had done some writing along the way. Then one day, a new director took over, and the organizational unit where I did my work was "reorganized," and my own work was threatened in the process.

To make a long story short, I scrambled to get out and was very fortunate in being offered a good academic position outside the government. The point I want to make here is that that reorganizational turning point was a very emotionally negative experience for me and a threat to my core self-identity as a scientist and bio-behavioral researcher. Moving from a governmental organization to an academic institution enabled me to fit back into a world of values, goals, and expectations where I had made my home since graduate school. At the level of rider, I shifted my social, cultural context at that point in order to maintain some kind of *horizontal* coherence in my life story—from past self to future self in a world of scholarship.

Jerome Bruner stresses that the main function of self-story is to explain, to justify, to morally persuade the listener (including myself) of the sense, the rightness, the reason for one's actions taken . . . to make sense out of events that stand out from the background of the ordinary. Such events can be joyful, surprising, shocking, deeply moving, and in many cases, threatening for one reason or another. As Teilhard says, "passivities" are the things that happen to us, negative losses, bad turns in the road, events that loom on our horizon that need to be reckoned with in one way or another. If you recall our discussion of his theology laid out in *The Divine Milieu*, God's presence can be found even in these negative events if we cooperate with God's grace-filled world surrounding us. We'll look at what that positive cooperation might look like in chapter 2 and beyond.

So, good stories can be written that produce growth and transformative thriving in the aftermath of traumas and even disasters. But let me point out again right here that not all stories—even very coherent ones—are good. Some stories are very consistent and coherent across a lifetime and their fruit is poisonous evil.

As I write this, the Times Square bomber—the young man who obtained explosive training in Pakistan and attempted to kill innocent American citizens, including women and children, by blowing up a van—proudly proclaimed his guilt in court. He said he would repeat the act in a heartbeat if he had the chance. He made it clear that his intent was revenge for the killing of innocent civilians by our soldiers in Afghanistan.

Now I expect that his attempted revenge act was entirely coherent—both horizontally over the years since he had become radicalized by terrorist indoctrination, and vertically, perfectly consistent with the "elephant's" assumed world of meaning and motives, as well as coherent with his goals and values narrated in his life story since adolescence. (I didn't assume coherence with his trait characteristics because if you remember, traits have little predictive value in terms of actual behavior. He could have been neurotic or not, introverted or not, friendly or not, but probably close-minded and rigid, and probably dutiful.) Paul Eakin refers to such a bad story as an example of "hypernarrativia." He says, "Narrative can destroy identity,"[18] enabling the storyteller to live out a fiction of destruction.

Eakin also refers to what he terms "dysnarrativia," where the "extended self" of memory and future expectancies is lost. Conditions such as Alzheimer's and various dementias are examples of brain disorders that rob the self of the ability to make overall sense of the world within any kind of coherent and continuous self-identity. Yet he also stresses that even so, there remains a core self, a grounded "hereness," the interpersonal self who can still relate in the present to others in their environment. But any sense of self as agent in a world of meaning with a past and future is gone.

But for the rest of us—neither terrorist extremists nor afflicted with dementia—there are good stories and then there are not so good stories. And what's the difference? According to Dan McAdams, a good story is coherent yet complex enough to be interesting—that is, not so coherent that it reflects no growth or dynamic change from crib to grave. Thus, a good story is open to and can creatively incorporate new experience. It is also credible (having some correspondence to what others can see as realistic and consistent and authentically reflecting the "facts on the ground"), extends beyond the self's sole interests, incorporating larger purposes in one's life; and in the face of trauma and loss (or Teilhard's passivities) a good story is transformational and redemptive in some sense.

Turning points in ones life can prompt the storyteller (that rider) to do some rewriting and expanding of the plot line in an unfolding life. For me, the turning points I referred to earlier in this section had to do with threat to my identity as a researcher,

18. Eakin, *How our Lives Become Stories*, 120.

and then a growing dissatisfaction with academic life and a search for a reconnect with basic religious values inherent in my sense of past self. Both life's victories and defeats as well as day-to-day surprises call for stories to be written—in one case whole life stories, and in other cases, smaller episodes that need to be explained and incorporated into the self's social world.

There is no doubt about it: negative, traumatic events threaten your sense of a coherent self and your assumptions about the meaning of life. But on the other hand, they are powerful triggers to rewrite the tale, to grow and transform yourself in the process. In the next chapter concerned with various practices that enhance life's flourishing, I'll describe in a bit of detail some concrete steps that can be taken to rewrite and transform your life story as you create your life's opus in midlife or later. But I'll just say here that a number of psychologists and other researchers have shown that when people confront their own life's traumas and reconceptualize these events into coherent and meaningful narratives (a process greatly aided by dialogue with others in community), they experience growth and flourishing as a result.

As Dan McAdams has said, in the midst of a secular, pluralistic world, in "the midst of this existential nothingness, we are challenged to create our own meanings, discover our own truths, and fashion the personal [stories] that will serve to sanctify our lives."[19] He says, "The stories we create influence the stories of other people, those stories give rise to still others, and soon we find meaning and connection within a web of story making and story living. Through our personal [stories], we help to create the world we live in, at the same time that it is creating us."[20]

But it is my assertion here that we not only make meaning in our lives, but that life *has* meaning that can be revealed, and thus discovered; that the world is permeated with God's grace and purpose. All three of the world's great monotheistic

19. McAdams, *The Stories We Live By*, 34.
20. Ibid., 37.

religions—Christianity, Judaism, and Islam—embrace this truth. And the prime function of a religion's stories and rites is to supply the symbols that carry the human spirit forward, to provide our lives with an ideological setting for the narrating of our own personal life stories. This religious worldview supplies the largest framework within which our stories are told.

As Teilhard puts it, we make our own soul through all our earthly days. We make our own selves within the bonds of a community of others who nourish and shape us dynamically in dialogue and in acts of meaning.

> Like an artist who is able to make use of a fault or an impurity in the stone he is sculpting or the bronze he is casting so as to produce more exquisite lines or a more beautiful tone, God, without sparing us the partial deaths, nor the final death, which form an essential part of our lives, transfigures them by integrating them in a better [story]—provided we lovingly trust in Him. Not only our unavoidable ills but our faults, even our most deliberate ones, can be embraced in that transformation, provided always we repent of them. Not everything is immediately good to those who seek God; but *everything is capable of becoming good.*[21]

And so we tell our stories, creating a coherent and meaningful whole in the process.

Let's turn now and consider the role of concrete practices—both individual and communal—which help us achieve that human flourishing amid all the goals we pursue and all the losses that befall us across our life course.

---

21. Teilhard de Chardin, *The Divine Milieu*, 86 (italics added).

2

Embodied Practices and the Flourishing Life

We are seeking a spiritual formation that, in its essence, is not about individual effort but communal action involving a spirituality of physicality, centered on the way we lead our lives, allowing us to be Christian in and with our bodies and not in our minds and hearts only; a spirituality of dialog within communities where the goal is not acquiring knowledge, but spurring one another on to new ways of imagining . . . a spirituality of creativity where creative gifts are not used as content support but rather as an invitation . . . to participate in the generative processes of God.[1]

So states Doug Pagitt, pastor of an experimental Christian community located in Minneapolis, Minnesota. Solomon's Porch community is part of what is loosely referred to as the Emerging Church—an amorphous, worldwide movement of local churches or gatherings, really a *Zeitgeist* that has spread from the United Kingdom, countries in western Europe, Australia, and

1. Pagitt and the Solomon's Porch Community, *Reimagining Spiritual Formation*, 32.

New Zealand to the United States in recent years. These gatherings or alternative churches that attract seekers of all ages, but especially the young, share many common values or principles (some of which we will look at here), but the spirit of the movement is reflected in the above statement by Pagitt.

As I was preparing to write this chapter, I was struck by two things. First, in reading much of the literature from this movement, I was energized, excited by what is happening in these renewal gatherings. Not that there is nothing to criticize, and we'll get to that in the pages ahead. But the wedding of embodied worship forms and artistic expression to the wisdom of ancient and orthodox tradition is pouring life into communal gatherings and feeding whole lives in the process.

The second thing I was struck by while reading the Emerging Church literature is how its emphasis on creativity and co-creativity with God complements Pierre Teilhard de Chardin's theology expressed in his *The Divine Milieu*. Each life is made up of what one does and what one suffers, what one actively creates and what one deals with along the way and in the end. We are called, each one of us, to develop our life to the full, and in the process God presses in on us, seeking to enter our lives in all circumstances directly sought or not.

For Teilhard we are indeed embodied souls, shaped by our God-given evolutionary past and molded in this life by culture and context. But that context continues to be created. Like Pagitt's vision expressed at the beginning of this chapter, we co-create the world along with God. Starting with our embodied self, you and I are called by God to build a work, an *opus*, shaping our own soul through all of our earthly days. For Teilhard, in cooperating with God, we join our life's *opus* with God's, contributing our life's creative piece to God's kingdom coming on earth. So nothing excellent is lost in the end. "Creation continues and we serve to complete it—even in our humble works." For Teilhard, nothing is profane in this God-drenched world where God is "at the tip of my pen, my spade, my brush, my needle . . . of my heart and of my thought."[2]

In the end, we are called to fashion our self in God's creative image and we are to grow through the works that challenge us. And so throughout this chapter as we focus on embodied practices that can undergird a flourishing life, you will see my turning again and again to what has energized me about the Emerging Church movement. In fact, this emerging spirit is the "glue" that holds this discussion of embodied practices together. So let's begin.

At the end of *The American Paradox*, David Myers draws some behavior change principles from psychological research. Two of these are particularly important for what we are going to be discussing here. The first is embedded in his statement: "What we do we gradually become." If you hang out with bad folks and do bad things, you gradually become a bad person. If you do evil things—molest youth, kill innocent others—you become less then human, you become an evil self. In contrast, if you join yourself to others who lead good lives, if you emulate and mimic their behavior, if you shape your behavior after saintly models, you become a better person in the process. Again, what you do you gradually become. Borrowing from the metaphor of elephant and rider, the rider's self-identity develops from the elephant's behavior over time.

This is a sound psychological principle. There is a whole history of psychological practices and therapeutic techniques built on this premise. There is also a long tradition in the wisdom of Judeo-Christianity that reflects this behavior change principle. Perhaps it is most succinctly put as, "praying shapes believing." Leaders in the Emerging Church movement say, "Try it on, try it out. See how it fits." And in the trying on, we become something new.

The second principle for embodied behavior change is conjoined with the first: community shapes individual lives. The practices we learn in community do shape our behaviors; at the most

2. Teilhard de Chardin, *The Divine Milieu*, 84.

basic, embodied level, such practices also shape our brains and thus our conscious attention to the world about us.

Myers also talks about the phenomenon that he calls "group amplification." By this he means that the power of the group amplifies the behavior of individuals embedded in that group. If you join a radical movement, your radical tendencies will become more so, will amplify over time. So if you already dislike Hispanics and you then join a vigilante group patrolling our southwestern border, you are likely to become more aggressive against illegal immigrants crossing that border than if you encountered them as an individual informant. On the other hand, if you join a life-affirming movement, your growth tendencies will be amplified. If you are struggling as an individual to overcome an addiction, you will find yourself empowered to resist it by group amplification when you join the local AA chapter.

And of course, since the embodied self and the community are finally inseparable, these two principles will guide our discussion of all the practices we will consider here. Turning to these practices, let's consider in turn first embodied prayer practices, followed by embodied expressions through singing, dancing, and ritual. We'll also take a look at the practice of telling stories in community and in the process, creating our lives within a religious context. We'll end the chapter with a look at the coherent life and the works of service as blessings bestowed on the wider community.

EMBODIED PRAYER PRACTICES: IN COMMUNITY WITH GOD

Doug Pagitt, the pastor of Solomon's Porch Community in Minneapolis comments on the physicality of certain prayer practices. He says,

> One of the most exciting aspects of this pursuit of physical expressions of faith is the use of the body as a means of prayer. It's fascinating to me that physical postures—kneeling, raising our arms, placing our palms up—can lead our thoughts into

a deeper state of prayer and meditation. In this process, the
mind comes under the reign of the body in a way that cannot
be forced but seems to come from a genuine connectedness
between what we do and what we think . . . Using our bodies
allows us other portals into the experience of prayer.[3]

One of the interesting little facts that I ran across in my reading of
the evolutionary neuroscience literature is that we humans have
inherited a tendency to kneel, to bow, to "make ourselves small"
before the face of superior or divine power. Other animal species
also crouch, turn belly-up, make themselves vulnerable in physical
ways that express surrender and "supplication" (if one anthropo-
morphizes a bit).

And so the prayer posture of supplication—of abasement, if
you will—comes naturally to humans and is universally found across
cultures. Thus since our bodies speak meaning to our conscious
selves, when a posture of "making the self small" is assumed, it naturally gives rise to a sense of being in the presence of Transcendent
Power. In Rudolf Otto's *The Idea of the Holy* he refers to this response
as a sense of tremendous awe and mystery before the divine.

It's impossible of course to separate off such embodied prayer
practice involving posture from other ritual behaviors, whether
accompanied by prayerful words or not. For example, making the
sign of the cross or anointing with oil are both ritualistic symbols
formed by cultural meaning. They are also essentially embodied
practices that express a spiritual sense beyond what words can say.
However, if there's no meaning behind the action, the ritual behavior seems awkward. But then again, as leaders of the Emerging
Church say, "try it on and see how it feels; you may grow into it,
the meaning might grow gradually from the practice." The process
of change and growth is a dynamic and bidirectional one, from self
to community and back to self as agent. And the brain is sculpted
by such practice.

3. Pagitt, *Reimagining Spiritual Formation*, 73–74.

Pierre Teilhard de Chardin reminds us that you and I are responsible in a sense for shaping our own souls (without intending any dualism here—it's just the way we refer to our spiritualized selves). We can do that by way of the communities of practice we embrace, the prayer experience we open ourselves up to, to what—in short—we pay attention to. In their *The Spiritual Brain*, Mario Beauregard and Denyse O'Leary ask whether adult human brains (and thus experience) can change. And they answer: "If neural circuits receive a great deal of traffic, they will grow. If they receive little traffic, they will remain the same or shrink."[4] To reiterate, it all depends on what you pay attention to and it is your self (that rider) who does the deciding . . . by which decision in turn, you alter your brain circuitry. They say, "For a [mystical experience] to occur, the spiritual self living at the core of each individual must also be willing to dance, so to speak."[5]

Beauregard and O'Leary have studied extensively the prayer phenomenon they refer to as RSME (or revelatory, spiritual, mystical experience)—the direct experience of encountering God in our deepest, conscious selves. They list as "triggers" to such experience meditative prayer, natural beauty, fasting, some authentic forms of worship—and more prevalently in other cultures, drumming, dancing, singing. All of these practices can open up a sense of the Divine Presence. It's interesting that they identify drumming, dancing, and singing as triggers to spiritual experience of God in other cultures but not so in ours. However, as we shall see in the next section of this chapter, those are just the triggers that have been resurrected in many of the emerging alternative worship communities.

In order to change your brain, and thus your experience of our world of meaning, you must pay attention. Frequently referred to as "mindfulness," or "quieting the mind," such focus of attention acts like a gate opening onto God. In her work *Train Your Mind,*

4. Beauregard O'Leary, *The Spiritual Brain*, 34.
5. Ibid., 266.

Change Your Brain, Sharon Begley suggests attention to Scripture, prayers, "thought, meditation, and other manifestations of mind can alter the brain, sometimes in an enduring way."[6] You and I are not stuck with the brain we are born with. She has the following to say: Genes set up brain regions to process auditory, tactile, and visual input. "But genes can't know what demands, challenges, losses, blows the brain will encounter [only an experiencing self living a life in community can know that] . . . [Nature has] equipped the human brain, endowing it with the flexibility to adapt to the environment it encounters, the experiences it has, the damage it suffers, the demands the owner makes of it. The brain is neither immutable nor static but is instead continuously remodeled by the lives we lead."[7]

When you think about it, these neuroscientists' assertions about the plasticity of our brains place enormous responsibility on each of us to tend our brains by tending to our practices within the communities we choose. So let me say a bit more about actual prayer practice before we turn to music and ritual, dance, song, and storytelling within an optimal social context.

There are so many, many books on the market that talk about how to pray. I don't want to simply repeat all that here. In an appendix to this volume, I will mention a few helpful resources, and in my previous book, *Imagination and the Journey of Faith*,[8] I also discuss forms of prayer and give a detailed list of resources for the reader to consider.

One of my favorite spiritual writers is James Martin. His *The Jesuit Guide to (Almost) Everything: A Spirituality for Real Life* contains a couple of excellent chapters on prayer (particularly his chapter seven—"God Meets You Where you Are").[9] Because Martin is a Jesuit priest, his emphasis of course is on Ignatian

6. Begley, *Train Your Mind, Change Your Brain*, 160.

7. Ibid., 130.

8. Levy, *Imagination and the Journey of Faith*.

9. Martin, *The Jesuit Guide to (Almost) Everything*.

prayer forms (St. Ignatius Loyola was the founder of the Order in the sixteenth century). Ignatian prayer is grounded in contemplation and meditation, particularly focusing on scriptural passages that lend themselves to imaginative engagement.

Among other forms of prayer, Martin details what is called *lectio divina*, or divine reading of Scripture. The meditative steps for this form of prayer usually include reading, musing over the meaning of a passage, taking it in, "chewing" on the content, letting it speak to you (what is God saying to me through this text?), responding in your own words, and then putting into action insights drawn from the encounter.

As Martin and others have pointed out, at heart our engagement with God in prayer consists of looking at God while God looks at you and me. Such engagement becomes a real meeting between persons—one small and fallible; One Transcendent, all powerful yet merciful and loving. One listens, one attends; one is silent finally in the face of Divine Presence. And in the process, the brain becomes attuned to the "sound of sheer silence"—the silence that becomes presence in and through us.[10]

EMBODIED PRACTICE IN RITUAL, DANCE, AND SONG: THE COMMUNITY AT WORSHIP

Doug Pagitt describes the music making that goes on in Solomon's Porch as the people gather for weekly worship. "For us music is not understood as preparation for learning, it *is* learning. It is not a precursor to worship, it *is* worship. It is more than a cognitive slide show of hopeful escapism. It's one way that we physically express our faith. *For us worship is not fantasizing about somewhere else but an attempt to create a place of physical participation in the life of God with our bodies, in a place, with a certain group of people and a very real God.*"[11] The songs are all written by members of

10. Bloom, *Beginning to Pray*.

11. Pagitt, *Reimagining Spiritual Formation*, 55.

that church and are thus contemporary forms of traditional faith embodied in vocal and group expression, vitalizing worship and bonding the community.

It turns out that our capacity to move rhythmically and respond emotionally to music and dance is a universal characteristic of human beings, an inborn capacity "there in the body, waiting to be brought out and developed, like the basic principles of language formation . . . Words remain quite inadequate to describe the nature of music, and can never diminish its mysterious hold upon our minds and bodies."[12]

In short, we got rhythm! And we are born that way. Because it turns out that our distant Neanderthal ancestors about 1.8 million years ago, having migrated into hot and humid parts of the African savannah, learned to stand upright, or in more technical terms, developed bipedalism, in order to catch the cooler breezes! "Stand tall, stay cool!" They also shed most of their body hair for the same reason.

But the Neanderthal's skeleton shifted in the process, among other things allowing the larynx to elongate and move down lower in the throat—affording a greater range of vocalizations beyond earlier "grunts and barks" as Stephen Mithen puts it. Their upright posture also required a larger brain to coordinate upright movement, which became rhythmic in gait, allowing them to run long distance, to jump, and to dance. Still living in small groups or tribes, this early ancestor had no need to develop complex, nuanced language communication. So they continued to express emotion and signal information holistically, using vocal and bodily gestures to greet, warn, appease, and so forth, manipulating others' responses in turn. They also expressed social meaning through rhythmic dance displays, vocalizing or singing rhythmically to sooth the young, and so on.

In his *The Singing Neanderthals*, Mithen stresses that the importance of bipedalism for human evolution cannot be overemphasized.

12. Mithen, *The Singing Neanderthals*, 278.

Then and now rhythm is essential to efficient walking, running, and complex coordination of bipedal bodies. Thus, the evolution of mental mechanisms to maintain rhythmic coordination of muscle groups contributed to the development of the human brain. "Many, if not all, of music's essential processes can be found in the constitution of the human body and in patterns of interaction of human bodies in society."[13]

For various reasons that we don't need to go into here, about two hundred thousand years ago our evolutionary line split off, and our own species, *homo sapiens*, came onto the scene. Living in greater numbers, these ancestors of ours developed the need for a more refined, nuanced communication pattern as groups enlarged beyond the small tribe. Language developed allowing ever greater evolutionary complexity and fitness—and the Neanderthal line became extinct. But important for us today is the fact that while we inherited separate capacities—for rhythmic, holistic expression in musical form from our Neanderthal ancestors, and for language expression allowing abstract reasoning to develop from our own *homo sapiens* line—we still retain that inherent capacity for making music and dance. "Infants are born musicians," Mithen asserts.

One of my earliest memories (probably not my actual memory but the memory supplied to me by family story) is me as an eighteen-month-old, standing out on our front lawn in Charleston, South Carolina, where my father was stationed in the navy. And I remember—or so I am told—that I stopped passing cars by the dance I was performing on the front lawn. My mom always referred to it as the "hoochy-coochy"! The family joke goes that she wondered where my dad had taken me so that I could have learned such a dance. But reflecting on that old family story, I know where I got that dance. I inherited it from my pre-human ancestor line. I was born a dancer! And so are we all.

Think of the last time you heard great, spirited music—say, the Celtic music from the show *Riverdance*, or Bruce Springsteen's

13 Mithen, *The Singing Neanderthals*, 139.

"Born in America," or the song "Tequila" (am I dating myself?), or Bizet's "Habanera" from the opera *Carmen*, or "Seventy-Six Trombones" from *The Music Man*. I bet you at least tapped your foot to that music's rhythm.

When we hear rhythmic music and when we dance in groups, we do tend to move with the beat for good reason. It turns out that there are motor paths in our spine and brain that trigger bodily movement to the rhythms we hear and dance movements we see. We become entrained to the beat and we move our feet in response. Mithen says that all music begins with a stirring of the body. He also adds that to feel with the body is probably as close as anyone gets to resonating with another person.[14] Music and dance tend to bond us with one another.

Alas, because language is so dominant in our Western culture as the preferred form of communication, this inborn capacity for music, dance, and song that you and I have inherited lies fallow for the most part—perhaps even a lost, holistic language of its own. Not only does language expression dominate, but also Mithen argues that the world of music appreciation and music making has become reserved for a professional elite—the critic and the educated musical aficionado. There is an elitism to classical music appreciation, and the world is divided into highbrows and low-brows—the latter the music of the street, the former the music of the concert hall. But music is music. And so Bach is one form; and the Beatles (sorry again to date myself) is another.

Although music is a universal human phenomenon, of course musical context, as well as expression is culturally diverse. Mithen points out that in fact the only universal *context* for musical expression is a religious one. Because religions deal with the "irrational," non-material, spiritual, unseen Reality, music—along with other rhythmic expressions such as dance, ritual, sacrament—become the chief means of grasping for, worshiping, and communicating with the divine.

14. Mithen, *The Singing Neanderthals*, 153.

Music, coupled with ritual, also triggers a cascade of "feel-good" neurochemicals (for example, endorphins and serotonin). And as it turns out, adolescents and young adults are particularly sensitive to such brain chemical surges. So maybe it's also not surprising to find so many young persons are attracted to alternative worship communities such as Solomon's Porch. Perhaps the young and seekers in general living in our highly mobile, pluralistic and culturally diverse culture, especially need such community bonding that these churches foster. These communities provide the anchor of meaning in otherwise unmoored lives.

In fact, religious gatherings of all kinds also function as "brain soothers." The person recognizes familiar faces with their welcoming (usually!) and reassuring expressions. Social signals such as forms of dress, as well as familiar music, reassure the participant that he or she is a member of the group; for others, symbolic expressions of making the sign of a cross or placing a scarf over the head reflect belonging. The atmosphere is positive and soothing, the music bonding. "The human equivalent of a positive signal, such as an extra-friendly smile with an extended and friendly focus or a hug conveys to the recipient that he is important a member of our group, respected, and worth attention—religious social moments can be hotbeds of conviviality. Signals elevate a recipient's sense of status, which is associated with feeling at ease and comfortable physically, mentally, and socially, as well as in charge of one's behavior. Accompanying positive socialization are chemical events that brainsoothe."[15] Given the "brain soothing" effects of the familiar faces and the communal ritual of church attendance, I guess it's not so surprising that even main line churches are still attended by folks on a regular basis.

And before anyone accuses me of throwing traditional, mainline churches under the bus, let me hasten to say that many denominationally affiliated churches are thriving. Later in this chapter, I will discuss two Episcopal churches as vibrant examples

15 Feierman, *The Biology of Religious Behavior*, 130.

of worship and outreach practices. Beyond my own denomination, there are worship communities ranging from black Baptist to Eastern Orthodox—and everything in between—that are thriving. Many incorporate exquisite, spirited music along with rich, embodied ritual, allowing participants to worship in and with their bodies, and not in minds and hearts only (to paraphrase Pagitt).

But in many cases other mainlines are dying. Something has been lost along the way. Our innate capacity for spontaneity and joyful exuberance, our bodily yearning for expression of deep meaning and communicating with God in some holistic and creative manner is not being nourished or enhanced in many places of worship. The church experience has become lifeless and rote, and attendance—especially among the young—has significantly eroded.

Which brings me back to Solomon's Porch and the use of contemporary and creative music forms to speak to seekers in this postmodern and postevangelical world of emerging religious communities.[16] And maybe given our evolved musical genes, it's not so surprising that religious faith is first discovered in such a community by folks actively participating in an emotionally evocative ritualistic expression. Recent biographies of well-known writers such as Mary Karr[17] and Sara Miles[18] describe just such a faith founding. First the experience of being swept up into ritual expression, following over time by a dawning religious belief embodied in a tradition they happened onto as adults. They tried it on and discovered that it fit—and they embraced it.

I think it's important to emphasize that in these experimental worship communities, there is a continued engagement with traditional orthodox belief (in this case, Christian) and ancient

16. The use of the term *postmodern* refers here to a cultural turn toward other avenues to truth beyond reason (for example, aesthetics); the more recent term *postevangelical* refers here to a theological movement away from rigid dogma and literal Scripture interpretation to a more dynamic openness to ongoing revelation within a pluralistic context.

17. Karr, *Lit*.

18. Miles, *Take This Bread*.

ritual, albeit not dogmatically or rigidly adhered to in any un-thinking way. That is, there is a "postmodern" understanding that all knowledge is perspectival and culturally situated. There is an understanding of biblical revelation as genuine but open to con-tinual dynamic interpretation. There is a respect for traditional interpretation, but an unwillingness to shut the door on growth in meaning through dialogue.

And of course as we've been emphasizing in these pages, there is a willingness to import and join with this ancient tradition contemporary cultural forms of aesthetic expression—from visual art, electronic media, modern dance, and dramatic performance, to contemporary street music. "Without tradition there would be no Christian faith . . . [A] 2000-year-old tradition gives a real sense of 'weight,' a much-needed anchor point in the world." It provides a check on individualism and heresy. But tradition "is living, not closed and completed . . . *To preserve a tradition then is to understand what is at its heart and then re-present that in our own context.*"[19]

As an example of "re-presenting" tradition in their own contemporary context, in their work, *Alternative Worship*, Jonny Baker and Doug Gay (along with Jenny Brown) describe forms of experimental liturgy in an alternate worship community based in Sheffield, England. They discuss the use of computer graphics, juxtaposing contemporary cultural images with ancient poetry or scriptural passages, as well as contemporary dance by all in the worship service. They say, "It was 'normal dance,' 'real dance' as opposed to churchy dance. This was perhaps more like a non-Western use of dance in worship—people were dancing in church in the same way as they would dance in a club or at a rave. This forceful introduction of dance to worship, in its 'unbaptized' and 'profane' form, brought with it a whole set of questions about physicality and the body . . . These were questions in search of theological answers."[20]

19. Baker and Gay, *Alternative Worship*, 147 (italics added).
20. Ibid., 21.

I have to confess that some of the alternative worship forms—the experimental liturgies attempting to wed traditional symbols of belief with contemporary music and movement—appear to me rather gimmicky. If I walked into a Sheffield bar to attend a Saturday evening worship involving ballroom dance or the draping of scarves dipped in ashes, I would personally disengage from the experience. (In my psychology days, I once attended a spiritual "retreat" at a northern California conference center where we stood in circles and passed rubber balls back and forth while we chanted something I quickly suppressed! I felt nothing but silly.) Still, it is clear from the Emerging Church literature that many twenty- and thirty-somethings find such contemporary expressions deeply meaningful and on the whole, such forms of dynamic worship appear to enliven the faith expression of many.

So in sum, embodied forms of worship found in modern and symbolically meaningful expressions of ancient belief nourish something in us that is inborn and thus, deeply human. The communities, both secular and sacred, which are rediscovering the expression of meaning beyond words are recapturing that "something that was lost" in last century's emphasis on reason and dogma. And the churches that are discovering this fact are thriving and attracting young lifeblood for the faith; those that are closed to such embodied, contemporary creations and expressions of meaning are dying out.

TELLING STORIES AND THE CREATION OF MEANING: EMBODIED PRACTICE IN COMMUNITY

In the first chapter, we considered the meaning of being human—holistic creatures who make meaning in part by the life stories we tell. Building on that discussion, let's look at storytelling in community—particularly religious communities—as a central practice in making a coherent life. The little story below was written by a homeless guy who was part of a writers' worship begun in 1993 in the Church of the Holy Apostles, an Episcopal Church in the area of Chelsea in New York City.

Only in New York

Things that happen here can be seen in the ordinariness of everyday life. In the daily lives of subway people opening and closing doors on a subway, the sanitation workers, a traffic guard. There are simple kindnesses that you find only here.

I remember helping a little kid across a street. His mother was on the child's left side. I was on the right. When the light turned to green, the youngster lifted both hands—one for Mom, the other hand for me. This may not sound like much, until you realize that I was a total stranger. I knew neither the parent nor the child.

The child, in simple fashion, grabbed his mom and me. After all, I was an adult. Wasn't I? All three of us crossed the street. The mother was a bit embarrassed but the child was not. We all three got across in fine spirits. Safely. Only in New York.

"Unless you become as little children, you cannot enter the Kingdom of God." Trust. One day at a time.[21]

The journalist Ian Frazier, who writes regularly for the *New Yorker*, received a grant to set up an arts program as part of a non-profit community organization of his choice. Frazier convinced the staff of Holy Apostles to work with him in offering a workshop for participants to write stories out of their own lives and share them with one another and the public as desired.

And for many of the 250 or so participants who have cycled through the worship process over the years the experience has been life transforming. Frazier says, "It's satisfying, too . . . to write a self-revealing cry or shout and lay it out for people to see, and to find patterns and beauty even in pain. Writing can be a kind of trampoline that bounces you higher until you glimpse the

---

21. McLoughlin, "Only in New York," in Maxwell and Shapiro, *Food for the Soul*, 109.

possibility of never coming down. It's one of the noble acts humans do, and almost always it ennobles those who do it."[22]

Referring back to our metaphor of elephant and rider, it's the rider who pulls the story together. But the story is grounded in the elephant's history—its development over a lifetime of experience—its culture, both given and chosen, which supplies that menu of symbols and story lines from which the rider chooses. And one peak period for putting the story altogether to achieve some kind of coherent self-identity is in adolescence and early adulthood.

As we discussed in chapter 1, stories are made and not simply found. The stories that emerged out of the Holy Apostles workshop—subsequently published under the title, *Food for the Soul*—were written in a setting that supplied symbols that carried spiritual and religious meaning. Of course, those homeless folks who volunteered for the project brought their own life experience, their own search for meaning, to that gathered community. That workshop gathering supported them over the weeks of telling their lives to one another. So the process was one of dialogue and communal shaping over the time of their meeting.

In some of the Emerging Church alternative gatherings, story telling also becomes part of the communal experience. In Pagitt's Solomon Porch Community, Sunday worship provides a space for "telling one's story," not an evangelical "Testimony"—although sometimes that is what is offered—but a sharing of a narrative piece of a life. Pagitt says:

> We all come with one [a story], participate in each other's, and are part of God's, so it makes sense to incorporate these stories into our community life. We invite people to share their stories, to listen to someone else's, and to allow the story of God to provide a better understanding of both.
>   . . . There are times when the story is explicitly about things of faith and times when it is about struggles or successes . . . While not sounding like "testimonies" in the traditional sense, these stories of the ways God bubbles up in others' lives serve

22. Maxwell and Shapiro, *Food for the Soul*, xviii.

as testaments to who God is and how God acts in our lives.
Telling and hearing these stories shape us and form us.[23]

As Pierre Teilhard reminds us, we shape and reshape ourselves in
response to life events and surroundings both that we choose and
that also befall us. And the story isn't finally finished until our last
breath. But as I've said before, there are good stories and then there
are not-so-good stories—stories that are open to new experience,
credible, and coherent; and stories that are stagnant, rigid, cynical,
and hopeless. Why are some stories better than others? In a sense,
this is another way of asking our prime question: why do some
lives flourish and others do not?

Ian Frazier said that writing and thus telling your story is
like jumping on a trampoline—you jump higher, you transcend,
you survey the whole and see the patterns laid down by piecing
together the entire fabric of your life. Even not-so-good stories can
be rewritten. But perhaps they can't be rewritten until they are told
and thus, laid out to examine and revise.

And this is where a community becomes essential. You can
talk to yourself, but frequently that is just a way to dig a hole deeper without finding a way out. But through some kind of dialogical
sharing, sharing with one other such as a "soul friend," or sharing
in a group like Frazier's workshop, perhaps a more coherent and
hopeful story can be written. Since meaning is created through
dialogue, our reality becomes constructed in large part by social
exchange.

There is in fact something powerful about sharing your story
with another person. And I do say that as a psychologist and former therapist, as well as a pastor. I also say this as a human being,
as one who shares her story with those three close friends over
lunch at our favorite restaurant.

So find a soul friend. Find someone who will listen to you
sympathetically, and will help you view the bigger picture of your
life. Who will affirm but will also hold up a mirror to what they see.

23. Pagitt, *Reimagining Spiritual Formation*, 56–57.

In his *The Stories We Live By*,[24] the psychologist Dan McAdams has developed a detailed conversational outline to follow in uncovering and understanding your life story in the company of a companion willing to listen to and explore your imagined "Big Picture" with you. Probably your spouse or partner is a bit too close to you to bring any objectivity to the conversation. But a good friend or a trusted and skilled pastor or rabbi would fit the bill. And also find a community, your own Solomon's Porch or Holy Apostles, find a community you can fall in love with, that will support the piecing together of your life's meaning through your own re-created story. Your re-imagined story becomes lived out in light of the community's own sacred story given in Scripture and song.

In answer to my question, 'What is a good life story?' let me refer back to the four criteria I discussed in my last book, *Imagination and the Journey of Faith*.[25] In brief, a good life story, one consistent with a religious sense of overall purpose and meaning in the one life God calls you to, is one embodying future hope and moral truth (for example, affirming equality between genders and races). A good story is also rooted in a tradition's wisdom, and is open to God's revelation in everyday life—in nature and in artistic expression. Thus, life stories expressing despair, racism, nihilism, and a closed or shut-up solipsism are in need of communal transformation.

And since in all lives, including your life and mine, losses and setbacks, sicknesses and reverses—Teilhard's "passivities"—happen, perhaps it's particularly important to look at what we tell ourselves about such dark moments. Because these inevitable losses threaten our sense of coherence and our assumptions about life's meaning, they can also provide springboards for building resilience, for personal growth, and for self-transformation. That topic, in fact, is the subject of our next chapter.

---

24. McAdams, *The Stories We Live By*.

25. Levy, *Imagination and the Journey of Faith*.

COHERENCE AND ACTS OF COMPASSION

In *The Long Loneliness*, Dorothy Day—the lay Catholic founder of the Catholic Worker Movement—writes, "We have all known the long loneliness . . . and we have learned that the only solution is love and that love comes with community."[26] So maybe this is a good way to stand back and reflect on acts of service as blessings that flow from a coherent, flourishing life.

Tony Jones reflects on what it means to act out of a coherent life base, for the elephant and rider to live in synchrony, to live out a communally shaped religious belief in a largely secular culture. He says, "most human activity is inherently theological, in that it reflects what we believe to be the case about God . . . So theology isn't just talk . . .Virtually everything we do is inherently theological. Almost every choice we make reflects what we think about God. There's no escaping it."[27] Integration and wholeness—coherence—is one of the hallmarks of the new Emerging Church movement. Service to the wider community, along with inclusiveness and hospitality, is another.

Two centuries back, Alexander de Tocqueville famously wrote about the manifestation of raw individualism in the American psyche. He said, "a calm and considered feeling that disposes each citizen to isolate himself from the mass of his fellows and withdraw into the circle of family and friends; with this little society formed to his taste, he gladly leaves the greater society to look after itself."[28] Or as my dad would joke, "I got mine; how you doin'?" And individualism still runs strong in our culture wars. Witness the growth of the tea party movement as I write this. Perhaps the complexity and competitiveness of urban living exacerbate such individualistic tendencies in us all. (The only time my neighbors

26. Quotation from Day's *The Long Loneliness* in Elie, *The Life You Save May Be Your Own*, 189.

27. Jones, *The New Christians*, 106.

28. Quoted in Myers, *The American Paradox*, 162.

speak to one another is when the power goes out and we step from our houses to ask each other why!)

But counter to that individual isolation is our need for one another, a universal human seeking after each other's company, a desire for relatedness, a longing for Dorothy Day's love that comes from community. And based on this human universal gravitation toward community is a sense of solidarity with others who may be different and "other" on the surface, but still have a common human bond with us, nonetheless.

This sense of solidarity with our own kind in need can be strengthened by community-imparted values. In fact, religious communities are a prime source of such moral values—as someone has said, supplying a reason to behave even when no one is looking. And it is at this level that acts of service flowing from grateful hearts become blessings bestowed on the wider community.

"When we participate in acts of service, we are stretching our faith to make sure it fits the world we live in. If our faith can't move us to feed someone who is hungry or help a single mother find shelter, it's simply not useful in the world."[29] Earlier I spoke about the Church of the Holy Apostles in New York City as a living example par excellence of embodied service to the wider community in need. Beginning in the recession of the 1980s, the Holy Apostles soup kitchen now serves upward of 288,000 hot lunches a year, as well as providing ancillary services such as a legal clinic, a medical van service, HIV outreach workers, and the writer's workshop we looked at earlier.

Holy Apostles' community outreach is absolutely inclusive, reaching out to not only Christians, but Jews, Muslims, and atheists; young and old; transvestites, homosexuals, college graduates, street people, and "others who never thought they'd eat in a soup kitchen." "Welcoming that diversity has had an impact on the parish that is palpable. We have learned to be open to people and ideas

---

29. Pagitt, *Reimagining Spiritual Formation*, 147.

that seemed inconceivable before. It stretches us and our faith,"[30] writes Elizabeth Maxwell, the associate rector of Holy Apostles.

After a devastating church fire in 1990, the sanctuary was re-built with no pews breaking up the space. The "guests" at the noon meals are invited to sit in that sanctuary to dine. "The diners seem to feel comfortable here, to know it as their place too. I believe the beauty of the space adds something to the meal, whether those eating are consciously aware of it or not."

> The meal we serve during the week stems directly from the meal we share on Sunday morning. In that meal we believe that we are fed with the very love and life of God, a love that is breathtaking in its boldness and vulnerability, its willingness to embrace every part of our human condition. As we gather at the table we remember Jesus, who spent much of his time eating and drinking with friends who included the outcasts of his day. We recall sacred stories of hospitality, loaves and fishes, a mysterious stranger recognized when bread is blessed and broken. In church, we share food, and we tell stories.[31]

At the other end of the country, out in San Francisco, an-other church opened up its doors and its sanctuary to all in need in the larger community—no passing of a litmus test required. St. Gregory's was an experimental liturgical community, fairly insular in its function, until Sara Miles turned up one day, wandered in, got swept up in the liturgy, and despite a lifetime of atheism or just plan nonbelief, had a profound conversion experience following ritual participation in the Eucharist.

To make a long story short, Sara Miles singlehandedly con-vinced the church to start a weekly soup program, and pretty soon the sanctuary itself became the place of welcoming and feeding of souls as well as bodies. Miles is a professional writer, a journal-ist (as well as a lesbian mother living with her long-time Jewish partner in the Mission District of the city). Overcoming initial resistance in the parish to such a feeding program (although Miles

30. Maxwell and Shapiro, *Food for the Soul*, xii.

31. Ibid., xiv.

insists it's not a program, it's a ministry of service, period), she turned the congregation upside down and inside out, stretching their faith in the process. She says:

> We were making church. "Church of the One True Sack of Groceries," Steve said. "'The Jesus Christ Love Shack," I said, "and House of Prayer for all, alleluia."
>
> . . . Just as St. Gregory's encouraged lay people to serve as deacons in its liturgies, at the pantry, the people I thought of as "pantry deacons"—our volunteers—weren't a select or professional group . . . They were more often than not misfits: jobless or homeless or a little crazy or just really poor. They'd stand in line for weeks, then one day ask if we needed a hand. The next week, they'd show up early, and the next, they'd be redesigning our systems, explaining to me how things could work better. Little by little, these new volunteers were beginning to run the pantry.
>
> . . . Each of us, at some point, might have been rejected for being too young, too poor, too queer, too old, too crazy or difficult or sick; in one way or another, cracked, broken, not right. But gathered around the Table in this work, we were becoming right together, converted into the cornerstone of something God was building.[32]

I don't know what your response is to all of that, the outreach service ministries at Holy Apostles and St. Gregory's, but I can't help but feel that that is church the way it ought to be. After all, as Doug Pagitt said, if our faith can't move us to feed the hungry, it's just of no use in the world. Of course, that's not all that the church is. But the point here is that embodied service is also worship. By this, I mean worship in the largest sense as a life of participation in the life of God with our bodies, our whole selves, in a place, with a certain group of folks and with a God who calls you and me to moral action.

Out of this communally shaped and fed experience can emerge a certain coherence to our lives in the deepest sense—a connection with the deepest levels of our personality, our need

---

32. Miles, *Take This Bread*, 134, 139.

for safety and for community, our need for connection and for real purpose in our lives. After all, individual coherence from our evolved core selves to our cultural embeddedness is not all that finally matters. (As we saw in the case of the times Square Bomber, evil lives can also reflect coherence.) The good lives that we choose and fashion, and the transcendent purposes that we finally embrace, matter in the end. The flourishing life as both God's call and our goal can only be achieved when the right choices are made that shape our coherent selves toward our proper end. And when these right choices are made, when we engage in prayer and ritual and communal story that in turn shape our lives toward the good, there are biological and psychological effects that follow.

Studies have shown that the intentional cultivation of compassion, through a life of prayer and conversation and communal shaping, does effect brain function and probably structure.[33] And in such acts of compassion—whether they occur in the experimental laboratory or in the street in front of Sara Mile's church or at the altar that has become a food preparation table—sacred food for holy people—we glimpse God's kingdom as coming into the world. Frederick Buechner says we cannot make God's kingdom happen because finally only God can accomplish that. But "we can put out leaves as it draws near. We can be kind to each other. We can be kind to ourselves. We can drive back the darkness a little. We can make green places within ourselves and among ourselves where God can make the Kingdom happen."[34]

33. In her book, *Train Your Mind, Change Your Brain*, Sharon Begley reports a study where the brains of monks were compared to the brains of college students when both groups were confronted with someone in seeming distress. The monks' brains showed less neural activity in regions of the brain that differentiate self from others (lowering the self/other boundary), making them more ready to assist the distressed stranger than were the students. When confronted with seeming suffering, they were ready to act and such readiness registered at every level of their selves, from brain to behavior. They were coherent, holistic responders from their core, conscious whole selves in their acts of compassion within that laboratory setting (236–37).

34. Buechner, *Secrets in the Dark*, 122.

In the pages ahead, we'll return to kingdom living when we address the topic of resurrection life and the flourishing self. But we can end here where we began this chapter, with Teilhard's thoughts about a soul-making response to God's call to be and to grow. By "developing our activity to the full, God presses in on us and seeks to enter our lives"—just as he presses in on the Sara Miles of this World. Teilhard prays, "To your deep inspiration which commands me to be, I shall respond by taking great care never to stifle nor distort nor waste my power to love and to do. Next, to your all-embracing providence that shows me at each moment, by the day's events, the next step to take and the next rung to climb, I shall respond by my care never to miss an opportunity of rising."[35]

---

35. Teilhard de Chardin, *The Divine Milieu*, 79.

Prologue 2

Three Lives

L IFE IS a terminal condition, as they say. We're on the road to our end. In the meantime, what counts is what we make of what we've been given. Some comedian or other asked, "Are you going to get any better, or is this it?" It's a kind of funny line, and I've used it on occasion or two. But it's funny in a way because at some level it rings true. I think it raises a question that maybe we all ask at some point. Is this it, or am I on the way to becoming some better person in the end? And what you and I have been given along the way to that end are both good times and bad, joys and sorrows—both well and woe, in biblical image—Pierre Teilhard's notion of "activities" and "passivities" in life.

Teilhard says the former—our freedom of choice, our will to accomplish and shape ourselves in the process—is a tiny "radius of light." This shaping of ourselves through the contexts we choose and the practices we embrace has been the subject of our first two chapters. But beyond this small radiance lies darkness and mystery. Teilhard says that this darkness is "the night of everything that is within us and around us, without us and in spite of us,"[1] to which we react because we undergo such uncontrollable events.

1. Teilhard de Chardin, *The Divine Milieu*, 75.

But the darkness we undergo can become our context of growth and transformation.

There are many givens which you and I do not choose: our genetic predispositions, our temperaments and traits. These are given and shaped by our cultures, but they are not finally chosen by us. But in addition, there are diminishments along the way that are not recoverable. Teilhard points out that we all have natural failings and weaknesses, physical defects, intellectual and moral limits and frailties which limit our field of choices. And of course, in the end, we grow old and then we die . . . one way or another.

Teilhard urges us to flourish as best we can. He calls us to grow and fashion our very selves—our embodied souls—through our reaching toward the good, resisting the evils that befall us. So when our way is blocked, we are to channel our activity along another fruitful path. When we face loss, we are to search for meaning which can redeem it. When we become ill and finally face death, we are to surrender this self which we have fashioned to the full over a lifetime—surrendering ourselves into the hands of God who hollows us out making room for Himself—breaking the "molecules of our being so as to re-cast and re-mold us into new life."[2]

Teilhard concludes his thought by asserting that this new life and final flourishing—this final victory of good over evil—will not occur until the eschaton or end time. You and I will not see this final victory in our present lives, but "the world, in which we shall live again, triumphs in and through our deaths."[3]

But in the meantime, his point for us here is this: If you have not done everything in your power to flourish in your lifetime, you will not be able to hand over to God as much as you might have been able to—if you had struggled to make your life as meaningful as it could be along the way. And recalling my study with retirees at mid- and later-life described earlier, apparently some succeed

2. Ibid., 89.
3. Ibid., 85.

in this struggle better than others. Hemingway once said, ""The world breaks everyone and afterward many are strong at the broken places."[4] Many . . . but not all.

In his work, *Making Loss Matter*, David Wolpe poetically notes that "each person, with age, builds or closes down rooms in the soul. Some people's capacity for love grows; others' shrinks."[5] Along with Pierre Teilhard, Wolpe does see life's vicissitudes and struggles as opportunities for growth—in some genuine way, the only real opportunities we have to achieve some meaning beneath the shallowness of hollow convention. Quoting John Keats, he asks, "Do you not see how necessary a World of Pains and Troubles is to school an intelligence and make it a Soul?"[6]

As a rabbi, Wolpe is naturally steeped in Jewish tradition. And he notes that the Torah—the Bible's first five books—ends with the death of Moses before he could reach the promised land. But then Jewish custom directs the people to turn back to Genesis and start reading again the story of creation—reminding those who read and pray Torah that death precedes creation, that death leads to life. He says, "We live in temporary homes as we travel through the wilderness. Nothing is permanent, and no place ideal. Our task is not to gather in the shade of the garden's trees, but to grow as we hold hands through the wilderness. The journey is made bearable, even wonderful, by community and by faith."[7]

As a concrete way into this discussion, let me introduce you to three of my good friends—two of whom I have lunch with regularly. The third one is now dead, and I never personally knew him (no lunches there), but I came to know him intimately through his wonderful autobiographical writing. These three—Philip, Charlie, and Anita—are exemplars of the flourishing life in the face of life's passivities, life's losses along the way.

4. Quoted in Viorst, *Necessary Losses*, 260.
5. Wolpe, *Making Loss Matter*, 141.
6. Ibid., 179.
7. Ibid., 38–39.

~

I never actually met Philip Simmons. I wish I had. But I did come to know him through a series of beautiful autobiographical essays he wrote under the title, *Learning to Fall*. I read this little book during a summer's vacation in upstate New York, and as we were driving home, the newsperson on National Public Radio announced that the writer Philip Simmons had just died. I felt like I'd lost a friend.

When Simmons was just thirty-five years old and an associate professor of English at Lake Forest College in Illinois, he was diagnosed with ALS (or Lou Gehrig's disease). He was told at that point that he had about five years to live. He outlived that prediction, and over the subsequent ten years, he set out on a spiritual pilgrimage in search of life's deepest meanings. His essays—which I have now read more than once—are not about how to die, but about how to live a flourishing human life in the face of all the sadness and loss along the way.

As his physical disability increased, Philip and his family moved from their Illinois home. He returned to his childhood roots in New England, building a house with a cabin where he continued to work on these essays, a house near his parent's home in the small New Hampshire town of his childhood. As the disease progressed, his life space shrank from climbing mountains to wheeling in a chair to the end of his driveway . . . on good days.

And yet. And yet. The amazing, indeed astonishing, fact is that for all of his loss, Simmons considered himself "lucky." He says, "I am the luckiest man on God's frozen earth . . ." despite the fact that his life had turned out to be not quite what he had had in mind. He had had in mind a long teaching career, along with an outdoor life of winter mountain climbing and summer diving off of a high rock into a flooded quarry near his childhood home.

But his life did not turn out that way . . . and come to think of it, probably your life and mine are turning out to be a bit (or a whole lot!) different than we'd planned at the start. And maybe that's a blessing. Simmons says that our lives as they unfold twist and turn in surprising ways. And of course, they're never finally finished . . . never finally settled until we die. He says, "the only thing that will settle the affairs of this life is death itself. To be settled in this life is . . . to die while still living, to live in sort of death-in-life. Only so far as we are unsettled is there any hope for us. Let us remain unsettled, therefore, in order that we may truly live."[8]

In an essay titled "Getting Up in the Morning," Simmons tells the story of a big old mama box turtle, who—after laying her nest of eggs (which was quickly emptied by a local caretaker to prevent their discovery by hungry raccoons!)—struggled and strained for hours to dig her way up the side of a deep, sandy ditch where she had crawled to deposit them. Seeing her struggle against the odds, she seemed to Simmons at that moment to be a metaphor for all the sisyphian struggles of our lives. And yet . . . she finally made it out . . . crawling toward the swamp from which she came, as if saying, "See? See how I dance? See how it's done?" She persevered despite all the odds against her. And Simmons reflects:

> I can survive. And, being human, I know more: Not only that I can survive but that I am blessed. Each day that I can get out of bed in the morning, I am blessed. Each day that any of us can move our limbs to do the world's work, we are blessed. And if limbs wither, and speech fails, we are still blessed. So long as this heart beats, I am blessed, for it is our human work, our human duty, finally to rise each day in the face of loss, to rise in the face of grief, of debility, of pain, to move as the turtle moves, her empty nest behind her, her labor come to nothing, up out of the pit and toward the next season's doing.[9]

Few of us have started off as mountain climbers with the whole world at our feet and wound up unable to button our shirt or tie our shoes . . . but all of us have been slammed with an occasional fastball that we didn't see coming. And I for one am astounded

8. Simmons, *Learning to Fall*, 44.
9. Ibid., 23.

at Simmons's gift of gratitude for life's blessings while—like that mama turtle—crawling and clawing his way up the ditch that his life has become. "See how I dance!" And I want to emulate him. I want to say "Me too." His beautiful prose inspires me to reflect on God's gifts in my life . . . all along the way. Again, in Simmons' own words:

> To thank God for broken bones and broken hearts, for everything that opens me to the mystery of our humanness. The challenge is to stand at the sink with your hands in the dishwasher, fuming over a quarrel with your spouse, children at your back clamoring for attention, the radio blatting the bad news from Bosnia, and to say "God is here, now, in this room, here in this dishwasher. Don't talk to me about flowers and sunshine and waterfalls: This is the ground, here, now, in all that is ordinary and imperfect, this is the ground in which life sows the seeds of our fulfillment.
>
> The imperfect is our paradise.[10]

It turns out that Philip Simmons has become an important person to me—despite the fact that he died several years ago. He has become my intimate hero—one of the beacons God has providentially blessed me with in my life of sometimes dark days.

I first met Charlie when I moved to Richmond. At the time he was Director and CEO of the Virginia Historical Society (VHS). A mutual friend had sent him a letter of introduction before I actually moved to this city, and after I settled in as rector of a midtown Episcopal church, Charlie invited me to lunch in order to welcome me properly to this Civil War capital. (When Virginians talk about "the war," they are referring to the late unpleasantness that ended in 1865, not the subsequent ones which have roiled our country since that great defeat.)

10. Ibid., 37.

One morning recently, Charlie and I sat in his new office chatting about his life. He'd left the VHS about a year earlier because of increasing disability with Parkinson's disease, which had been initially diagnosed in 2004. He and a friend had started up a consulting business last year, advising various institutions on organizational and financial matters. Their consulting firm had been amazingly successful in a short period of time. Their first year they had accumulated a dozen clients to advise and help weather the bad economy which had descended upon us all.

When I asked Charlie about any blessings that he saw stemming from his diagnosis with Parkinson's, near the top of his list was the gathering of a small group of fellow Parkinson's sufferers who had become intimate friends over the past five years. Because he had gone public immediately after diagnosis (unlike Michael J. Fox, who had tried to hide the disease for a decade—much to Fox's regret), over the last five years Charlie had become the public face of Parkinson's in the Richmond community. Like a magnet others were drawn to him for advice.

They've formed a support group that meets monthly over lunch. Originally there were four of them, and now they are up to about fifteen members who meet and "problem" solve for one another.

Charlie exclaimed, "I said, 'Look you guys! You don't have syphilis. You don't have to be embarrassed. You have Parkinson's. Don't try to hide it . . .'" We were sitting around having lunch. Someone said, 'We ought to call ourselves something.' I said, 'Movers and Shakers,' and that cracked everybody up. It was perfect. We're a support group and we get together for lunch once a month . . . We have a joke. In order to join you have to fail the shirt-buttoning contest."

In addition to problem solving and support for each other, this group of fifteen has now spearheaded the development of a Parkinson's research center here at the Medical College of Virginia, and have raised more than nine and a half million dollars in funding for that effort. So despite the fact that if Charlie had his "druthers," he'd have preferred to skip the diagnosis, nevertheless some concrete blessings in the form of close friendships and community development have flowed from that original trauma.

And trauma it was. He said, "at the age of fifty-seven, I was having a lot of pressure at the VHS . . . had to fire someone . . . tired all the time. Friends who hadn't seen me in a while noticed that I didn't seem like myself. So I saw my doctor and after describing what they had seen and what I'd begun to feel, he said 'You've either got a brain tumor, or had a stroke, or you've got Parkinson's. I think it's the latter and let's do some tests.'

"Two weeks later I was back with Cammy" (Charlie's beloved wife). "The doctor told us it was Parkinson's, and then he walked out of the room. We sat there and cried. My first response was to read everything I could get my hands on about Parkinson's. I thought, 'Oh, God, my life is over.' I was consumed with it . . . all I could think about. But I decided right away that I wouldn't hide this . . . told my board and staff right away. Inside I was scared, shocked. But you know . . . I never got angry, never said, 'Woe is me,' or 'why me?'"

Charlie told me that after a while the immediate shock wore off. He continued in his high profile position at the VHS for four more years. "I said early on, I'm not going to question why this has happened. This is not God's plan—hell, that helps a lot when people say that! I hadn't done anything. This is not [God's] revenge. I just have Parkinson's I can either shut down with life as I know it, or I can keep on going.

"I kept on going. I continue to exercise. I try to have as normal a life as I can. I made a determination after two-three months [after diagnosis] . . . It [the disease] is my enemy. By God, I'm going to fight it every step of the way. I'm not going to give in to it. It will eventually win unless some miracle comes along, but I will make it so hard on it. If I go into depression and whine about this, it will have won. I'm not. Him . . . he's my demon. I'm going to fight him by exercise, take the rights meds . . . have a good attitude."

In terms of the future . . . what lies ahead of him . . . Charlie is pretty realistic. He recognizes that Parkinson's tends to shorten the lifespan, but he hopes—with exercise and medicine and the support of his loving wife and friends—he hopes to live another twenty years, recognizing that at some point he and Cammy are going to have to look into a retirement or assisted living community. In the meantime, he plans to stay active, work another five or six years in his consulting firm . . . travel.

He said "I try not to think too far in the future . . . in my . . . Most people know you'll slow down with age. But with Parkinson's that process is accelerated. Sometimes I feel my age . . . I feel like an old man sometimes. When my meds aren't working the way they should. A lot of people with Parkinson's get depressed, withdraw. I'm not going to do that. If I would, it would win. I'm not going to let him do that to me . . . I'm going to stay active, positive as long as I can."

Reflecting back on our conversation, I was struck by Charlie's hope-filled grace in the face of this "last turning point" in his life, as he puts it, struck by his spirited resolve, his stamina shown throughout the years of his traumatic loss. I am deeply inspired by his hope-filled vision for his own life and the life of those he touches through the community bonds which he has forged. Where did such stamina, such spiritual resolve come from?

There were two great influences on Charlie's life and character—his mother and his grandfather. Charlie's father, a talented musician and composer who had given performances in Carnegie Hall, died suddenly of a massive heart attack in front of his eyes when Charlie was eight. His mother moved him and his sister back to a little town in Tennessee to live with Charlie's paternal grandfather. His mom had given up a life of glamour and excitement in New York to teach high school Latin and English in a small, conservative, "redneck" town in the South. Yet, despite the fact "she went through hell there," Charlie never saw her "cry or complain, or whine." He said, "And if she'd see me whining, complaining, she wouldn't have it. 'Don't feel sorry for yourself,' she would say. 'What good does it do? Don't feel sorry for yourself.' She never complained. And I think I got that spirit from her."

Charlie describes his grandfather—who lived fifteen more years after they moved in with him—as a Southern gentleman, a gentle man who "lived his religion, a southern Baptist. He'd lost his beloved son and two sisters and wife within a short period of time before we moved in, yet he never complained. He might say 'I'm a little blue today.' I can still see him sitting and reading his Bible every day."

Charlie's love of history really stemmed from his grandfather's story-telling, stories about the farm, stories about Civil War Union patrols taking their food. "He just brought it to life. He was a wonderful role model, and really inculcated in me an interest in history. He was a remarkable storyteller. I think it was this early love of history that led me to go to VMI" (Virginia Military Institute). And because of this love of history, Charlie's life course has unfolded as it has, bringing history to the public in the positions he has held throughout his career.

He concluded, "I am a most fortunate, lucky man. I've had a wonderful life. A strong marriage, two children who are a joy. My career has been a dream come true. How many people have a job tied to their deepest interest and dreams."

And as I said, for me Charlie himself is an inspiration—a hope-filled, indomitable spirit staring in the face of tragic loss. Like Philip Simmons, he has reached down into the depths of himself and has found a strength of soul—shaped initially by the primary models in his young life, a devout and gentlemanly grandfather who told him wonderful stories, a strong mother, and a great uncle who taught him to "treat everyone with respect." But Charlie has continued to evolve beyond childhood influences, shaped and inspired by historical models and nurtured by Baptist and Presbyterian communities along the way.

~

"I am the luckiest person in the world. I have been incredibly lucky in my life . . . blessed. I have lived an interesting life along the way, one incredible thing after another. Blessed with family . . . I adore . . . they love me . . . friends. As an AME minister once said, 'God has done alright by me!'"

This said by my friend Anita who—looking back over her life of eighty-two years (she looks ten years younger and has the zest of a fifty-something-year old!)—summed up her life for me as we sat across the table in her family room. This from a woman who lost her only daughter in childbirth; whose beloved first husband died a painful death from pancreatic and liver cancer after eighteen years of marriage, leaving her with three young boys to raise. This from a woman who lost the sight of one eye after contracting a disease caused by altitude sickness while piloting a small plane (more about that in a bit); whose second beloved husband died seven years ago from Alzheimer's disease, and whose middle son had a stroke in his fifties and is now quite handicapped. "I have been incredibly blessed in my life," Anita says over a glass of red wine we are sharing while a gentle rain falls outside.

First, here is a little biographical sketch. Anita grew up in New York City, the cherished only daughter of a Sicilian household. She had one brother, and apparently each of them thought for many years that they alone were the favorites in the family. She had a loving, secure, noisy, and demonstrative (after all they *were* Sicilian!) childhood home.

Anita married her first husband, Ken, at age twenty-one. "We moved out of New York City to a farm on the Eastern Shore of Maryland. We knew nothing about farming, had forty-four acres and did things like muck out stalls and feed the chickens. Ken was an engineer and had a city job, but the farm was the center of our life. It was a wonderful place to raise the children."

"Living on the Eastern Shore was small-town living. Being a city girl, I had never experienced that before. We made our own community as outsiders, a small community within a community near the town of Easton made up of Jews, Sicilians, and other 'damn city folks!' From 1957 to 1981 I lived there, and the community of friends we formed was tight knit. Our friendships—which still endure—were deep. Our bond was strong because of the unfriendly environment of this small town life."

Anita gave birth to three healthy boys while losing her one little girl during childbirth—the "deepest tragedy" of her life. After a few short years, Ken was diagnosed with serious malignancy, and the family lived with that knowledge and experience for a decade. Ken finally died while their boys were still young (spanning ages seven to fifteen). And for about two years after his death, she experienced "lostness"—floundering around and fearful basically of being an inadequate "father" for three growing boys, missing her life partner whom she had adored. She was in her late thirties during these "lost" years. She asked, "Do you remember the novel by . . . I think it was Wally Lamb . . . *She's Come Undone*? There was a song by that title, too . . . and I thought at the time they were singing about me. I'd come undone, alright."

This period of Anita's "lostness"—her "undoneness"—lasted for a couple years, and when I asked her what it was that pulled her out, she described a combination of factors: community bonds, church attendance, work . . . and the passage of time, as well as her indomitable spirit.

One of the cardinal virtues my friend exudes is openness to others, a fundamental hospitality, a welcoming into her home and life. But also in times of need, a willingness to reach out for community support. She said, "After Ken died, I sold the farm and moved closer into Easton itself. But the same community of friends was my mainstay. As more outsiders came in from other places, our circle grew. During that early period after Ken's death, I don't know how I functioned. I depended tremendously on friends. I joined every kind of support group . . . for the company, I guess. I was stubborn . . . never took the advice . . . I went for the conversation."

During her sons' growing up years, she describes their home life as a haven for hippie friends. "We were living in a household of hippies . . . it was wild . . . it was wonderful. There were always people in and out, coming and going. One summer we had a house full of kids . . . practically stacked like logs. We had a wonderful time!"

At some point during those years, despite being a Roman Catholic (struggling with the institutional Church, which many of us did in those days), Anita started also attending an African Methodist Episcopal (AME) Church. The congregation was mostly black, mostly poor. "But God how they would sing! These were the cleaning ladies, the porters, the waiters, poor blacks mostly . . . wearing clothes we had given to the Salvation Army. And yet . . . they praised God for all they had. They were joy-filled. It was mind blowing. Poor souls, thanking God in a way I didn't . . . appreciating the world in their lives in a way I'd never heard before . . . still saying 'thank you' with all their hearts. An hour and a half . . . two hours . . . and God how they sang!" So friends, community, church—these were the main anchors in her life which began to slowly turn around, when she began to get her bearing once again.

Being irrepressibly adventuresome, in her early forties and feeling more grounded, Anita decided to take it upon herself to learn to fly. Thought it would be fun! She had absolutely no fear of flying (which always impressed me because I'm not far from being white knuckled about it) . . . or fear of much else, for that matter. Unfortunately, just before she took her solo run, she was flying with her instructor and suddenly the earth below looked like "a Picasso painting. All I saw was fractured . . . fractured light . . . something was clearly wrong."

It turned out that she had contracted what's termed Eels disease, which happens to pilots due to lack of air pressure in the cabin, and she lost the sight in one eye. And to this day, Anita has no depth perception. When I asked if she found that devastating, she exclaimed "I could still see! I could read. I was only worried that the blind eye would shrivel like a raisin and I would be ugly. I was young . . . forty-two." Did she take it in stride, then? "What else could I do? And I could still see!"

When I finally asked her what the turning point was, Anita thought for a moment . . . and then responded, "life I guess. Happiness. I find it very difficult to stay unhappy for any period of time."

Anita met her second husband, Jonathan (a psychiatrist by training), in 1981; and after some moves, they came to Richmond, Virginia, where we first met in 1997. My husband and I were drawn into her circle and we have been close and good friends over the past decade.

Jonathan died of Alzheimer's disease in 2003, and shortly after that, her middle son, Peter, had a crippling stroke. But still, as we ended our conversation on that rainy afternoon, sitting across from each other and sipping a small glass of red wine for a little sustenance, Anita concluded, "I have no complaints. God has done alright by me. And you know, it's not good people that bad things happen to, bad things happen to everybody! You take them along the way. Accept them.

"Or you can bitch about them the rest of your life and make yourself miserable. There is something to acceptance. Life tosses you the proverbial lemon once in a while. You do the best with what you've got. It scares me when people don't accept the reality of life. In every life, darkness happens and it's not the worst thing. If you honest-to-God believe . . . that there is a next life. If you really believe it, then O.K. I'm ready to go. There is a time when it's acceptable to accept death, a natural end, natural beginning to another life."

Anita concluded that "in the meantime, life is filled with surprises and joys that maybe you can only appreciate the joy against the darkness. Appreciating the light against the black surround. There is a future. It may be not what I expect, but there is another life in another dimension. It's not something to be feared. It's going to be a good, a joy-filled one. Like I said. I am the luckiest person alive."

3

Creating a Flourishing Life through Suffering and Loss

KIERKEGAARD, THE Danish philosopher, said something to the effect that "crises are necessary for full human growth." And if you reflect back on our three friends here—Philip, Charlie, and Anita—you will notice that as life trauma overtook them, they each actively engaged in a struggle with their life's core meaning and were transformed—for the better—in the process. Each of them altered their life goals that they had been striving after; in the process, they transcended their daily experience by rewriting their stories in order to incorporate their loses, thus redefining the basic meaning of their lives.

Because Teilhard's "passivities" are part of every life, and because each of us is called to flourish and grow to our fullest self until our last days, such positive meaning-making and transforming growth should also occur through weathering all that happens to us in the meantime. In fact, in their work, *Trauma & Transformation*, Richard Tedeschi and Lawrence Calhoun stress that "for an individual to achieve the greatest psychological health [and thus flourish], some kinds of suffering is necessary."[1]

1. Tedeschi and Calhoun, *Trauma & Transformation*, 12.

A process of adaptation to life's loss has been studied and clarified by these and other researchers in the field of positive psychology. In fact, something like a natural course to suffering and growth on the other side of dark days and "lostness" has been traced in the works that we'll consider here. And perhaps you, like me, will also resonate with this natural cycle of crisis and transformation as you reflect on your own coping with losses along the way.

There's no doubt about it; when bad things happen to you, there are immediate negative consequences. According to Tedeschi and Calhoun, negative events (or again, Teilhard's "passivities") tend to be traumatic because they frequently catch us off guard; they tend to be out of the ordinary of our everyday lives, so we have no past experience or fund of wisdom to draw from. We consequently see ourselves as unable to control what is happening to us. And if the traumatic events are irreversible (such as being diagnosed with a chronic illness such as Philip's or Charlie's, or losing a child or husband in Anita's case), the impact on our lives is significant and long-lasting.

Consequently, such loss events initially prove shocking and cause a shift in our self-image—from one who controls ones life to one who is vulnerable and initially helpless. As we saw in Anita's and Charlie's stories, the immediate emotional impact is anxiety, "lostness," depression, and at times irritability and angry outbursts.

Well where is the good in all of this? Again, as we witnessed in my three friends' lives told here, over time many—if not most—persons can emerge on the other side of trauma transformed and even more perfected than before, gaining wisdom along the way. As Hemingway said, "The world breaks everyone and after which many are strong at the broken places."

Humans are amazingly courageous, and have the capacity to transcend adversity and flourish despite loss. I have seen this with patients that I have treated, and more recently with parishioners I have counseled who are struggling with crises. They rise to the awful occasions in their lives with amazing grace. But what does this transformation process look like—what's it's shape and what . . . or who . . . can facilitate it?

Tedeschi and Calhoun describe a process of recovery that can last months or even a year or two (remember Anita's "lostness" lasted about two years after her first husband, Ken, died). These researchers have identified three areas of growth leading to transformation and flourishing on the other side of trauma.

First, over time—after illusions of perfect control are broken—*an increased sense of self-reliance and personal strength* is often reached. Individuals who experience profound loss often discover strengths they hadn't known they had before undergoing the trauma. That was certainly true for me as I weathered my first life crisis dealing with the organizational reverses at the National Cancer Institute, described in an earlier chapter. And since then, there have been additional losses and "passivities" that have overtaken me in the course of living my life—most recently the death of my dear husband of thirty-five years, taken slowly from me by Alzheimer's disease.

In terms of the biographical sketches given here, maybe we can see this shift in self-image toward one of self-reliance especially in Anita's story. Perhaps we could say that a more realistic sense of personal strength—as well as vulnerability—leads to a certain mature wisdom and well-being over time. Good coping models (like Charlie's mom, for example) also aid in the recovery and transformational process. Models of strength, a community of support, and a conversation partner to assist in rewriting ones story are major sources of resilience and flourishing after loss.

Tedeschi and Calhoun describe a second area of growth and flourishing through crises in the sphere of *social relationships*. After losing someone who is dear to us by death, or experiencing other dark reverses in our life, often these researchers found an increase in compassion and empathy for other sufferers. They also saw an increased ability and willingness to express emotions and disclose limits and flaws in oneself. This is not always the case, of course. Some folks become bitter and withdraw from those around them. Some deaths, like the death of a child in the household, can actually drive people apart because of guilt and recriminations. But with the support of community and others who take the time to care, meaning can be found even in the darkest times based on a whole new or renewed philosophy of life.

And this is the third area of growth that Tedeschi and Calhoun describe in their work. On the other side of trauma, many who are able to flourish in a transformed way do so by making comprehensible what has happened to them by *creating meaning out of the chaos of their lives.* While some become cynical, it seems to be the case that the potential for growth despite loss is an inborn potential within all human beings. And according to these researchers, religious belief is a great aid to meaning making after trauma.

Interestingly, religious belief can provide a sense of *indirect control* over ones life in the face of loss by leaving in God's hands the mystery of suffering in our lives. But ultimately a religious tradition can provide a "Big Picture" of life as overall deeply meaningful. Such a horizon or worldview can make sense of what befalls us, giving meaning to our life as a whole—despite the awfulness that occasionally happens to us all. Tedeschi and Calhoun put it this way: "To prevent traumatic events from shaking the foundations of meaning, the individual's sense of purpose and value must be universal and enduring." And this "sacred canopy" of meaning can be supplied by a religious community—its rituals and stories shaping our sense of what is enduring and true.

As Tedeschi and Calhoun point out, the final step in giving meaning to trauma is to weave such tragic and sad events that befall all of us (exemplified in Philip's terminal disease, Charlie's chronic disorder, and Anita's several losses along her way)—to weave such "passivities" into our life stories—achieving a sense of overall coherence as we complete our life journeys. These researchers conclude that those who finally perceive growth as a result of trauma, struggle to cope initially, finally discovering meaning that enlightens them, incorporating these discoveries into a life path narrative that is satisfying and filled with pride.[2]

To summarize, there are positive biological and social effects when you struggle to live a flourishing, coherent life—where your embodied sense of what's worthwhile is fully consistent with the meaning you make of your life story—despite trauma and loss. Such coherent flourishing is finally fully complete when integrated with some community transmitted and shaped sense of God's presence and call in your life.

Turning to my three friends here, I find it likely that Philip, Charlie, and Anita brought to their episodes of trauma and loss certain resilient tendencies and the emotional wherewithal to fight against such loss, and flourish in the end. But I think they also demonstrated a willingness to fight against their setbacks and create new meaning by rewriting their stories against considerable odds. And they were transformed for the better in the process.

And in that transformation, each of them drew upon wellsprings of gratitude, hope, and even joy despite loss—increasing and deepening these emotional reservoirs as they did so. My point is that these evolved and inherited emotional tendencies grounded in your and my very humanness and embodied in our marvelous brain structures can be strengthened by practices that we have seen already—communally shaped rituals and stories embedded in a tradition's reservoir of life's meaning.

TRANSFORMING THE ELEPHANT: LIFE'S LOSSES AND POSITIVE EMOTION— GRATITUDE, HOPE, AND JOY

For our purposes here, I want to focus on three positive emotions: gratitude, hope, and joy. Undoubtedly all three of my friends found within their emotional reservoirs all three of these positive

2. Tedeschi and Calhoun, *Trauma & Transformation*, 41.

emotions, plus others besides—including at times "lostness," anxiety, depression and the rest of the negative emotional gamut that we all inherit as part of our biological equipment. But these positive emotions are—or become—predominant in each of their lives as they struggled against the dark and were transformed through the trials (the "passivities") that befell them.

Gratitude

The positive emotion of gratitude is a quiet feeling, but one with great, life-giving power. In his work *Twelfth Night*, Shakespeare's words reflect ancient disdain for those who do not express gratitude for gifts and benefits: "I hate ingratitude more in a man than lying, vainness, babbling, drunkenness, or any taint of vice whose strong corruption inhabits our frail blood." And in the world's monotheistic religions gratitude for God's blessings is a virtue to be praised.

As with other positive emotions, gratitude is both a momentary emotional response as well as a virtue or long-lasting trait. Psychologists working in the field of positive emotions list gratitude as one component of the universally found human trait of self-transcendence—that virtue that lifts us out of our own self-centered interest (that elephant again!) and bonds us to others.[3]

Thus, somewhere in our brains, gratitude resides as a definite, inborn potential. This is the case because gratitude itself—proper recognition of a good turn or benefit and the tendency to return the favor—probably evolved from our earliest primate origins for the sake of cooperation through social bonding. And in terms of this brain we have inherited from our early ancestors, it's likely that—as with all of the positive emotions—the midbrain emotion and memory centers, interconnected with the moral-judgment center in the forebrain, provide the neurological base for this

3. Peterson, "The Values in Action (VIA) Classification of Strengths," in Csikszentmihalyi and Csikszentmihalyi, eds., *A Life Worth Living*, 29–48.

emotion. Since gratitude expression has been found across all world cultures, this emotion does appear to be part of a spiritually evolved human nature.

Although this grateful tendency is inborn in our species, its expression is strengthened by the example of others. So by six years of age, only about 20 percent of children say thanks to an adult for a gift or favor; but by age ten, over 80 percent say thank you. In adolescence, as with most socially shared values, a willingness to see favors as benefits and to feel and express gratitude is greatly influenced by peers and mentors. Building on this evolved capacity, religious communities reinforce such grateful tendencies. For Jews and Christians, the importance of gratitude—of giving thanks to God in all circumstances—is part of our inherited tradition.[4]

Do you remember the lyrics to that old song that went something like, "When I'm worried and I can't sleep, I count my blessings instead of sheep, and I fall asleep counting my blessings"? Well, it turns out that there are good reasons why counting your blessings soothes you to sleep.

Barbara Fredrickson and her colleagues have shown that positive emotions generally, and gratitude specifically, operate as "mood repairers" when negative thoughts and emotions erupt.[5] For example, anger will most likely prompt you and me to engage in a narrow range of lashing-out behaviors. And when you're angry, your heart rate goes up, stress-related hormones are released via the sympathetic nervous system, and blood pressure rises. But it turns out that just the *memory* of an episode giving rise to a grateful emotional response short-circuits anger and its

---

4. And please note, given this inborn and universal tendency toward gratitude, a tradition's wisdom shapes and guides us to know what to be properly grateful *for*. Bin Laden was presumably grateful that the two planes collided with the World Trade Center towers. But the act itself and its result were evil.

5. Fredrickson, "Gratitude, Like Other Positive Emotions, Broadens and Builds," in Emmons and McCullough, eds., *The Psychology of Gratitude*, 145–66.

physiological effects. For example, cardiovascular recovery (or a return to normal heart rhythm) is enhanced by invoking positive emotions, including again the emotion of gratefulness for some remembered blessing.[6] As Barbara Fredrikson puts it, such positive emotions and their effects can transform individuals in an "upward spiral toward optimal functioning."

Despite being afflicted with a terminal disease, Philip Simmons says, "to thank God for broken bones and broken hearts, for everything that opens me to the mystery of our humanness . . . and being human, I know more: Not only that I can survive but that I am blessed . . . I am the luckiest man on God's frozen earth!"[7] From the depth of his trauma, Simmons still recognized the gift of life—surely an antidote to despair, as well as a reflection of flourishing in the face of (or because of) life's loss.

As with other positive emotions, beyond physical and spiritual benefits to the *individual* who expresses gratitude to others and ultimately to God for life's blessings, *communal* benefits also occur. People who appreciate life's benefits from others and ultimately from God, tend to want to give back to others from the largesse they have received. They seek out opportunities to give to others, and again such pro-social behavior bonds friendships and strengthens community ties. Researchers studying the effects of gratitude have measured what they call "elevation," or inspiration from another's generous self-giving.[8] Just the observation of gracious generosity (for example, viewing a film showing Mother Teresa's work with India's poorest) motivates the desire to be better

6. In one study, grateful individuals were found to have significantly lower posttraumatic stress disorder symptoms following trauma than individuals prone to be less grateful for benefits and gifts in their lives. So gratitude acts as an antidote to a negative emotion's physiological consequences, whether that negative emotion is anger, anxiety, or depression.

7. Simmons, *Learning to Fall*, 37, 44.

8. Haidt, "Elevation and the Positive Psychology of Morality," in Keyes and Haidt, eds., *Flourishing*, 275–89.

oneself, and to search for ways to give back and express virtuous, pro-social behavior.

Since some benefits—like life itself—cannot be repaid, grateful individuals will creatively search for new ways to repay such divine generosity. Such new ways for expressing gratitude (such as charitable giving, volunteering to help those in need, touching others and expressing loving regard) will therefore be found and followed. In Philip Simmons' case, he wrote his book, *Learning to Fall*, and in doing so, he gave back to untold others the wisdom he had discovered groping through the darkness in his own life's struggle. And I, for one, will always be deeply grateful for that gift.

In the end, practicing gratitude and developing the virtue of a grateful heart also lend themselves to kingdom building in the Judeo-Christian sense of that term. A desire to resist social evils and to create a more just and peaceable society is fueled by such "habits of the heart."[9] Although the world's major faith communities have also contributed their share of evil, at their best they have for millennia fostered and shaped such kingdom-building virtues. They have done so by encouraging our positive emotional tendencies rooted in our wonderful biological equipment, which allows such shaping and flourishing in our lives.

Hope

Hope, like the other positive emotions, is a blend of feeling and thought—as George Vaillant puts it, a blend of both poetry and prose. Poets and scientists alike have grasped for hope's essence, what hope consists of, what leads to it and what it offers humans as thy traverse their lives. The poet Charles Peguy imagines God saying,

9. But these virtuous or character habits, resting on the positive emotions and behaviors required for community building, must be shaped and learned within communities larger than a local subculture. This is so because local communities can be more easily shaped by the warped visions of their single leaders—such as Jim Jones or Adolph Hitler or Osama bin Laden.

> Now I tell you, says God, that without that late
> April budding, without those thousands of buds,
> without that one little budding of hope which
> obviously anyone can break off, without that
> tender, cotton-like bud, which the first man
> who comes along can snap off with his nail, the
> whole of my creation would be nothing but
> dead wood . . .
> But my hope is the bloom, and the fruit, and the
> leaf, and the limb,
> And the twig, and the shoot, and the seed, and the
> bud.
> Hope is the shoot, and the bud of the bloom
> of eternity itself.[10]

George Vaillant[11] writes that hope is "the capacity for one's loving, lyrical, limbic memory of the past to become attached to the 'memory of the future.'" St. Paul says, "hope is the belief in things not seen." Now where does such hope reside in the brain? Coupling reason with memory and planning, the comparatively large frontal lobes of the neocortex (which do separate us from the rest of the animal kingdom) appear to play a major role in supporting hopeful anticipation.

On the psychological level, such hopeful expectation does seem to predict resilience in the face of trauma, as well as better physical health outcome in a number of studies. For example, a hope-filled religious commitment expressed by cardiac patients reliably predicted longer postsurgery survival compared to matched patients without such hope. The same survival advantage was found in a study of inner-city, disadvantaged youth who were able to obtain an education and thus had reason to hope for a better future than their parents. Those who grew up convinced that

10. Peguy, "Hope," in *God Speaks*, 98, 103.
11. Vaillant, *Spiritual Evolution*.

they had something to live for simply lived longer compared to a matched sample of youth without such hope.

However, hope does not deny the truth. Nor is it mere empty wish or self-deception. I mean, we're not talking Pollyanna here. Neither Philip nor Charlie or Anita endorsed still upper lips or living a lie. They knew what they had lost. No, those who hope look unblinkingly at reality and still cling to what is not yet seen but positively anticipated—some good, some light to appear in the midst of the dark, some golden glimmer at the end of the tunnel. In fact, it has been said that you cannot hope without knowing the truth of pain or sorrow—like you cannot fully appreciate the good without knowing the bad. In other words (especially if you know Jesus's parable of the lost coin), you cannot rejoice in finding that coin unless you first experience the pain of its loss.

Hope does face truth embedded at times in darkness. Hope for survival of community and freedom rose from the ashes of the twin towers after 9/11. Nelson Mandela's release from prison after thirty years behind bars gave hope to millions. Barack Obama's rise to the presidency—whatever your political persuasion—gave hope to blacks in this country and to peoples around the world that individual achievement is honored and prejudice itself has lost sway in the free world.

Perhaps the absence of hope is reflected in a person living day by day, with no thought to future fulfillment. The opposite of hope is despair or maybe pessimism; its exaggerated state is reflected in a simple-minded, Pollyannaish personality, self-deceiving and unwilling to recognize the reality of suffering and death. But as we saw in Charlie's and Philip's lives, real hope looks death in the face, yet nevertheless hopes for further blessings in the meantime, and ultimately hopes for life beyond the grave.

So maybe for all three positive emotions that we are concerned with here—gratitude, hope, and joy—a proper balance is necessary, providing the proper ballast in life's journey. Like Zorba the Greek, one hopes, one plays, dances, sings exuberantly, one is grateful for blessings, maybe especially in the face of life's sorrows and losses. This is perhaps what it means to be fully human . . . to fully live a flourishing life.

What is the wellspring of hope and how can we enhance it in our own lives? Whatever its memory and emotional brain base, hope builds from the time of birth based on trust and nurture by a loving parent or surrogate. Hope can also be awakened later by giving a child a future through supportive mentoring and educational opportunity. As in the case of Philip and Charlie, hope can increase by recreating and retelling one's life story so that trauma and loss can be revisioned as redemptive turning points in one's life. Finally, hope can be built through community engagement and spiritual awakening within a worship context.

Joy

Like gratitude and hope, the experience of joy is also hard-wired into our ensouled bodies and frequently gets expressed through them in music and dance. Paleoanthropologists have identified flute-like instruments for music making as early as our Neanderthal ancestors over fifty thousand years ago, and probably before that new mothers cooed and sang to their infants. Kay Redfield Jamison puts it this way, "Music and dance are deeply embedded in the social character of our species. They ignite, infect, and express our collective, complex emotions: music and dance arouse group energies for the hunt, or planting; celebrate the seasons of the gods; and mark, thereby abetting—through communal festivals of passage into adulthood, marriage, and death—recognition of change within a group. To music we raise our armies and lower our dead."[12]

As Jamison points out, music acts quickly on the brain, focusing attention on the moment, narrowing the perceptual field to the rhythm of the communal body. She says, "the wide-open

---

12. Jamison, *Exuberance*, 156.

whirl of dance is a head-thrown-back joy, one that leaps away from life-weariness into a different world. Dance energizes and unites; it quickens, it exhilarates, it liberates."[13]

Within an individual's own evolution or development across the life course, the experience of communal joy or mutual engagement begins to develop by about two months of age when the limbic system neurally connects with the forebrain. Such neural connections underlie mother and child bonding in mutual embrace. As in our earliest ancestors, the infant begins to play with hands and feet, and the growing toddler explores the wonders that lie all about, while the adolescent engages in the rough and tumble of playful sport. The joy of creative movement and discovery is thus hard-wired in our human brains.[14]

This sense of joy also becomes a major motivational force in our lives, prompting those who have experienced joyful moments to seek such moments again. Unlike happiness to which we habituate after receiving some good or reward, we never tire of bubbling joy. So for example, if I get a promotion at work, I may feel very happy. But after a brief while this happy feeling wanes and I can hardly remember the honor! I was happy when my bishop

13. Ibid., 156.

14. Canadian neuroscientist Mario Beauregard and his colleague Denyse O'Leary carried out a series of brain studies on a sample of Carmelite nuns, expert practitioners of contemplative prayer. The nuns were brought into their laboratory, attached to sophisticated brain monitoring equipment, and asked to vividly recall past mystical experience.

After the experiments were over, the nuns reported experiencing intense joy at the memory of what they interpreted as divine encounters. But Beauregard and O'Leary also found that such recall actually triggered anew the sense of present joyful Transcendent union. And in Christian terms, such joyful bliss could be considered as a glimpse . . . a taste of God's kingdom.

These researchers also found that such intense mystical episodes leading to joyful experience were not in fact localized within any particular brain region (that is, no "God spot" was found), nor was brain activity during the episode confined to the temporal lobes, as one sees in some forms of epilepsy. We'll return to the whole question of spiritual self-transcendence and the question of divine encounter in the pages ahead.

named me regional dean, but then I discovered the drudgery of extra meetings, and somehow the happiness quickly evaporated! But in contrast, the experience of joy seeks over and over to repeat itself, and so—for example —I never tire at the return home of my loved sons now grown.

Further, joy is always a communal experience, whether it happens while caught up in dance, in family celebration, in a household like Anita's filled with your son's hippie friends, or ecstatic communion with God (see footnote 14). In contrast, episodic happiness is always situated within the individual him- or herself—my promotion is primarily mine alone, and can be celebrated without another soul to share it—and is always subject to satiation, habituation, and waning over time.

Just as you cannot experience hope without knowing the pain of loss, philosophers have recognized over the millennia that you cannot experience deep joy without knowing some sorrow along the way. As my friend Anita observed, how could you know what light was without a background of darkness? If you never had the experience of loss or the pain of saying goodbye to someone you love deeply, how could you experience the deep joy felt on their return? In addition to whatever evolutionary advantage the limbic-based positive emotions give us, perhaps most if not all of them—hope, forgiveness, love, compassion, gratitude—function as antidotes to loss and sorrow. Vaillant says that "joy is grief inside out," affirmation of life over death.

Now it is true that folks differ in capacity for joyful exuberance. Anita noted that it was impossible for her not to experience joy for any length of time. At the psychological level of temperament—of emotional tone tendencies that we are each born with—there is in fact a large genetic component. From birth some persons are just more prone to be timid and withdrawn, while others show early on a sunny disposition and an exuberant willingness to explore. Studies have repeatedly shown that identical twins, even those reared apart, are more likely than fraternal twins to show similar extravert or introvert tendencies. Studies have also shown that children who early on show behavioral inhibition will exhibit timidness is adulthood. In contrast, those children who are most talkative and bubbly and exuberant in play, develop into adult extraverts. High-energy children naturally become exuberant adults.

However, and crucial for us here, the relationship between the environment and an individual's developing temperament—or more generally, the relationship between the social and cultural world and the individual's developing brain architecture over a lifetime—is complex indeed. Kay Jamison concludes that "all animals are shaped not only by their genes, but by the circumstances under which they develop . . . 'Nature versus nurture is dead. Long live nature *via* nurture.'"[15]

And we do nurture one another, don't we? Or we could. I suppose we've all been in the presence of another who is just filled with the joy of living, an exuberant personality who is larger than life, who walks into the room and lights the place up. Joy, in fact, infects. Just as Anita radiates a sense of infectious joy wherever she goes, we are drawn into the orbit of joyful ones and are repelled by other's gloom and boredom. C. S. Lewis once wrote, "good things as well as bad are caught by a kind of infection. If you want to get warm you must stand near the fire; if you want to get wet you must get into the water. If you want joy . . . peace, eternal life, you must get close to, or even into, the thing that has them . . . If you are close to it, the spray will wet you; if you are not, you will remain dry."[16]

Summing up what we've said about joy, it's that positive human emotion that expresses a flourishing, creative zest for life. As an eighty-one year old poet once exclaimed, "You have to allow yourself to take joy. Otherwise, you're no good to anyone."[17] Joy can be caught from others, so choose your companions well. Joy can be experienced as the quiet thrill, the awe-struck gaze at a

15. Jamison, *Exuberance*, 112.

16. Quoted in ibid., 138–39.

17. "Fifty of the Most Inspiring Authors in the World," 50.

shower of stars across the night sky; joy can well up when you experience hearing Beethoven's Ninth Symphony, his "Ode to Joy." Joy is a life-enhancing emotion that both reflects and enhances human flourishing . . . an antidote to sorrow. "Nature teaches that joy can be replenished, life can succeed death, joy can find its way out of sorrow."[18] In short, exuberant joy defies evil and shouts, "Yes we can!" instead.

There's an infectious quality to being around someone who shows such positive emotions. But not only that. When we see acts of gratitude expressed as generous giving, or when we are in the company of a zestful, joy-filled companion, or when someone who has experienced tremendous loss nevertheless expresses hopeful expectation that something good can still happen in their lives, I think we are inspired to be and do likewise. We get a clear glimpse of living virtue, we understand at some deep level what gratitude, hope, and joy are in lives as imperfect still as our own.

TRANSFORMING THE RIDER:
LIFE'S LOSSES AND MEANING MAKING THROUGH
GOAL ADAPTATIONS AND STORIES

In the last chapter, we talked at length about how telling our stories creates coherent meaning in our lives. And in that discussion, I emphasized the importance of telling your story in community—at the least in dialogue with a sympathetic listener, and finally "in conversation" with a whole community's traditions and stories, a community's way of life. I'm not going to repeat myself here. But I do want to point out the crucial importance of re-writing ones life story in order to create new meaning out of the chaos of life's losses.

Referring back to our metaphor of elephant and rider, it's the rider who switches goals in the face of steep obstacles. And it's the

---

18. Jamison, *Exuberance*, 300.

rider who pulls the whole story together, giving new and perhaps wiser meaning after struggle with trauma.

Shifting sought-after goals can be a healthy, transforming strategy in the face of loss. Putting this another way, Teilhard says, "sometimes the check we have undergone will divert our activity on to objects, or towards a framework, that are more propitious."[19] If a career is lost through forced retirement, if sickness limits ones energy to climb mountains or run an institution, then turning to other options can be both liberating and lead to further flourishing. W. R. began to study Greek when his music career ended. Philip Simmons could no longer climb or stand upright to lecture to students, but he could still write essays that were gifts to the world. Charlie could no longer direct a major institution with its demanding personnel and financial responsibilities. But he could open a small consulting firm and spear-head fund raising for a research institute. These are real life examples of the rider deciding to switch life goals, enhancing holistic flourishing in the process.

Jennifer Pals, a psychologist who studies the remaking of life stories after severe life reverses, has focused on what she calls the "triggering effect" of traumas that erupt in and disrupt our lives. It turns out that folks are sometimes more and sometimes less successful in rewriting that narrative.

Pals studied transcripts of life stories told during a lengthy interview where participants were asked to reflect on the meaning of both high and low points in their lives.[20] She asked whether these life stories reflected growth and transformation or were these "trigger events" seen as having lasting and negative consequences—somehow contaminating the rest of their life story.

Because she was interested primarily in the process of meaning making after life trauma, Pals analyzed what she referred to as the "spring board effect" of negative experiences in these lives.

---

19. Teilhard de Chardin, *The Divine Milieu*, 86.

20. Pals, "Constructing the 'Springboard Effect,'" in McAdams et al., eds., *Identity and Story*, 175–99.

And it turns out that some of the folks she interviewed pieced together life stories that never achieved any kind of positive coherence, but rather reflected negative, depressive dead ends and overall lives of regret.

On the other hand, some told stories of triumph over adversity and redemptive growth through the losses they experienced. These latter were able to recognize and acknowledge the negative impact of the loss, showed active grappling with the meaning of the event thorough dialogues with self and others, and actively wove together new meaning of the negative event—connecting it with a positive sense of their selves as redeemed in some sense despite loss.

Even though Pals found that "dialoguing with the self" can be fruitful, in the end, talking only to yourself often leads to little other than digging a hole deeper without finding a way out. Tedeschi and Calhoun did consider that initially after a traumatic event, most folks need time to ruminate and muse about the meaning of what has befallen them before they can begin to construct new meaning for their lives. But that was only the beginning of the process of coherent reconstruction.

I cannot emphasize enough the importance of conversation with others as you put your story back together. Since meaning is created through dialogue, our reality becomes constructed in large part by social exchange. Such creative dialogue uncovers and makes explicit "what will come to be known in our saying it to someone who will reply."[21] If you remember Ian Frazier's beautiful metaphor, he says that telling your story to others is like jumping on a trampoline—you jump higher, you transcend, you survey the whole and see the patterns laid down by piecing together the entire fabric of your life.

So as I said before, even not-so-good stories—stories that end in hopeless dead ends and are filled with regret—can be rewritten once they are told, once they are laid out to examine and revise.

21. Quoted in Elie, *The Life You Save May Be Your Own*, 357.

And here is where community becomes essential. Much of this research I've been considering here leads to the following conclusion. Re-writing your life story within a religious community's tradition—given the power of a tradition's stories and rituals to lay the groundwork for the deepest layer of meaning in your life—can provide the best chance for creating a sense of coherent flourishing in the end.

Thinking back over especially Charlie's and Anita's stories as they pieced them together on the other side of trauma, they drew from their community's reservoir of stories and rituals that provided value, purpose, and meaning to the dark days in their lives. They created meaningful life stories with a religious sense of overall purpose in the one life to which God called them to flourish within, embodying future hope—open to God's revelation in their everyday lives. The life stories that all three of my friends knit together at this end of their journeys were very good indeed.

CONCLUSION

Somewhere along the line, somewhere in middle to later adulthood, all of us early to late baby boomers and beyond begin to look ahead to the time left for us, knowing that the years ahead will be filled not only with personal triumphs of one sort or another, but also realizing that as we age, inevitable loss and sadness will come our way. So even if generally healthy—and this generation is more fit than any before it—I think we still peer ahead and wonder about the quality of our lives over the next decade or two or three. We tend to stay younger longer and older longer (as I write this my mom just celebrated her one hundredth birthday!), and so the quality of how we live out the rest of our lives, the good times and the bad, matters more than ever. We begin to wonder at some level about how well we're living our life . . . or not, fearing that maybe we're just fidgeting it away, rather than flourishing to the fullest extent that we can.

Some of us perhaps were raised in a faith tradition that provided the answers that no longer speak to our everyday experience and the burdens we increasingly bear. And not only our personal burdens weigh on us, but the world's evil seems to erupt at increasing frequency. As someone has observed, you and I live on the cusp between skepticism and some deep awareness of positive Mystery beyond ourselves—despite the awfulness we see about us.

On the other hand, we are indelibly stamped by secular values, and our vision is shaped by our science-driven culture. So by reflex we doubt the reports of mystical visions, cynically (or realistically, we would assert) assuming mental derangement instead. And yet. And yet longing for something more, something transcendent, sensing that our childhood faiths calling us to a life of virtue and prayer might have been onto something after all. As David Myers captures in the title of his book,[22] we are "spiritually hungry people in an age of plenty."

In his *Making Loss Matter*, David Wolpe refers to a song in Lerner and Loewe's play *Gigi*, which included the line, "I'm glad I'm not young anymore." Whether the old man singing the song would actually refuse youth if it were offered again to him is a moot point because he doesn't get the choice, and neither do we. Wolpe asks instead whether "he will fashion something meaningful from his losses. Will he let the universe defeat him, or will he use loss by turning its own force to his advantage?"[23]

Lives of coherent integrity, both vertical coherence extending from the elephant's aims to the rider's life story, and horizontal coherence extending across a lifetime of narrative meaning based on memory and hope, are fashioned by selves in community. Meaning is created and confirmed through conversation and practice. And both despite, and because of our life's losses, we are called to flourish to the last day of sentient life. And by God's grace, we can.

22. Myers, *The American Paradox*.
23. Wolpe, *Making Loss Matter*, 113.

4

The Ultimate Flourishing
Resurrected Life and Kingdom Living

"WHERE IS my mother?" she wanted to know. "I just don't
know where she is. Where is she, do you think?"

Mary (not her real name, of course) sat in my office a week
after her mother's funeral, struggling with her mom's death and its
aftermath, struggling with her sense of loss left by the utter silence—
that profound sense of absence that the dead leave us in their wake.
I must have tried to say something reassuring, maybe something
about the communion of saints and the spiritual bond that we hope
and believe connects us still to our saints who have gone before us
into that life beyond this life of both joy and suffering.

But I didn't really feel what Mary was asking me out of the
depth of her grief until my own father—whom I was very close
to—died in 2001 . . . and then felt more acutely when Leon, my
husband of thirty-five years, died last summer, almost two months
to the day before my mother also died at the age of nearly 101.
Then I found myself asking the same questions that Mary had
asked more than a decade ago: Where is he? How is she? Is he
at peace? Does she still know me? Is he surrounded by love? Or

simply *is* she? How is my husband, my dad, my mom still a person, a self, without the loved body that once was them?

These are the ultimate questions, aren't they? Questions that humans have been asking for millennia about their dead, and about their own future beyond death. We humans have asked these fundamental questions about death and beyond since we first crawled out of the cave and evolved into creatures who are able to transcend our immediate surroundings and who can imagine and express through language and other symbols the images of an afterlife for our dead.

From the beginning of this book, and across all its chapters, I have stressed the nature of human being as embodied and holistic. From our brief look at the relevant findings from the fields of evolutionary neuroscience and psychology, I (and many others) have concluded that we are embodied souls or minds, with an evolved brain which allows cultural and social development over time. Such cultural evolution and its artifacts in turn sculpt and shape our individual brain's capacities for further creation, and for ecstatic engagement with other humans, as well as with God. Such has been our journey heretofore in this work concerned with human flourishing.

For most of our Western tradition we have stubbornly clung to the notion of bodily resurrection. Judeo-Christian tradition up until at least the seventeenth century never really broke ties with the notion of holistic embodiment and the final resurrection of human flesh at the end of time. Certainly Christianity has staked its very core identity on the idea of bodily resurrection. St. Paul says something to the effect that "if Jesus Christ was not raised from the dead, we are, among all peoples, the most to be pitied." Our faith rises or falls on the possibility that God did raise Jesus's embodied and transformed person from the grave on that third day—that first Easter morn—and we likewise will be raised in the end.

In fact, such belief is rooted deeply into our Judaic heritage. Although the bodily raising of one particular individual before the end time was not expected in Jesus's circle (hence, the puzzlement of his disciples when he spoke of his own death and subsequent resurrection), nevertheless deep in the Jewish Scripture was embedded the notion that at the last day, God would indeed raise up the righteous—both body and soul, or as embodied, whole selves—honoring God's long-awaited promise of life given in covenant to His chosen people.

Caroline Walker Bynum concludes her scholarly work *The Resurrection of the Body*[1] with the following caution: "To make body crucial to personhood is to court the possibility that (to misquote Paul) victory is swallowed up in death."[2] In a real sense, the notion of an embodied self as essential to human being and the belief in the promise of a resurrected and transformed, embodied person at the end of time is an all-or-none proposition. Either you are saved as embodied—or you will not be saved as the self that you necessarily are in the end.

As a footnote to her point, Bynum quotes a fragment from a lovely poem by John Updike that reads

> make no mistake: if He rose at all
> it was as his body;
> if the cells' dissolution did not reverse, the
> molecules reknit, the amino acids rekindle,
> the Church will fall . . .[3]

Thus, in a real and vital sense, the matter of this chapter is about life and death, and about our hope as human beings that God's promises of resurrected life are true. Either it is all true or none of it is. And as Paul says, in the latter case we are truly tragic

1. Bynum, *The Resurrection of the Body*.

2. Ibid., 343.

3. Updike, "Seven Stanzas at Easter," in *Telephone Poles and Other Poems*, 72

creatures—longing for final meaning and life beyond this life, longing for ultimate transcendence beyond this life of corruption and disease and death, but finally exiting this stage of fools as dust and nothing more.

It will come as no surprise to the reader that that is not where our journey together will end.

RESURRECTION IN THE BIBLE AND TRADITION: THE FLOURISHING LIFE AFTER LIFE

With respect to resurrection beliefs, it turns out that Christians and Jews share common scriptural and historic roots. In their work, *Resurrection: The Power of God for Christians and Jews*,[4] Madigan and Levinson argue that Jews and Christians should really be seen as "siblings" rather than as child issuing and superseding the parent, siblings with a common root regarding resurrection embedded deeply in the Jewish Scriptures, and further developed in later Talmudic and early Christian theologies.

But it is true that much of the Hebrew Bible (called the Old Testament in common parlance) has little to say about the dead, and certainly little to say about any sense of individual survival beyond the grave. When you were dead, you were dead, and that was it. Because individual identity was inseparable from the communal identity of God's covenant people, if there was any sense of one living on, it was in the sense of the community living on by God's covenant promise. That is, individual identity—in life, as well as death—was identified with the people of Israel. An individual lived on after death only in the sense of having offspring as part of a kinship community which would live on in a secure land of promise. Being without offspring or living in exile as disinherited and cut off from the land was equivalent to death. God honored God's promise of life in the survival of the Jewish nation. The self was a self only as relational and embedded in the people of God.

4. Madigan and Levenson, *Resurrection*.

Nevertheless, deep in the heart of the Old Testament lie hints of resurrected life prefiguring later notions of resurrection for the righteous in the end times. For example, the book of Isaiah, chapters 40–55 (referred to as Second Isaiah, the portion of the book written to Judeans in Babylonian exile) expresses hope for the reversal of national death by the return to God's promise of homeland. And even if you are not an Old Testament scholar, Ezekiel's vision of the valley of dry bones—of "'dem bones" knitting together, becoming enfleshed, and rising up again—is a vivid and memorable sign of God's final vindication of God's righteous ones in the end.

Referring to Ezekiel's vision, a later Jewish scholar some centuries after that book was written remarked, "If those who never existed (as in Ezekiel's vision) can come to life, those who once lived—all the more so!" Madigan and Levinson conclude here that "this reversal of national death anticipates the idea of end-time resurrection that appears only later in Jewish history."[5] And that resurrection was understood by the faithful to be as an embodied, resurrected state.

Despite the fact that for the most part individual identity was entwined with national identity in this early period of Jewish writing, nevertheless there existed even then a certain tension between an individual's biological death and God's promise of life. In fact, hints of individual longing for life beyond the grave can be found even in early Old Testament writings. As Madigan and Levenson point out, the Song of Hannah found in 1 Samuel 2:1–10 suggests that God's power to give life and heal extends beyond the grave, *not only to the people as a whole, but to individuals as well.* Hannah sings

> The LORD kills and brings to life;
>> he brings down to Sheol [a place of darkness for the dead unrighteous] and raises up.
> The LORD makes poor and makes rich;

5. Ibid., 146.

98

> he brings low, he also exalts.
> He raises up the poor from the dust;
>   he lifts the needy from the ash heap,
> to make them sit with princes
>   and inherit a seat of honor. (vv. 6–8a)

These authors conclude that in this relatively early scriptural writing the "Song of Hannah" hints that God's power to heal extends even to the netherworld and even for individual persons.

Within the late writings of the Hebrew Bible, the book of Daniel contains the first clear and unarguable prediction of the resurrection of the dead. Both the nation *and* the individual righteous will be resurrected to "eternal life." The writer of Daniel applies the older image of Isaiah's Suffering Servant (Isa 52:13–15) and that Servant's vindication ("See, my servant shall prosper; he shall be exalted and lifted up, and shall be very high"—despite suffering and death) to individuals who are found worthy of resurrected life. (Isaiah's Suffering Servant of course was seen by later Christians as a prefiguring of Christ.)

"There shall be a time of anguish, such as has never occurred since nations first came into existence. But at that time your people shall be delivered, everyone who is found written in the book. Many of those who sleep in the dust of the earth shall awake, some to everlasting life, and some to shame and everlasting contempt. Those who are wise shall shine like the brightness of the sky, and those who lead many to righteousness, like the stars forever and ever" (Dan 12:1–3). Here the vindication of the righteous nation is extended to both the individual righteous, as well as to sinful unrighteous, both experiencing their just rewards in the end. If Israel will only repent of its ways, then "they shall flourish like a garden; they shall blossom like the vine, their fragrance shall be like the wine of Lebanon" (Hos 14:7). Such an expectation of life beyond life, not only for humankind, but for all of creation, itself, passed over into late Jewish rabbinical teaching and then later into Christian belief.

By the second century BCE and extending to the destruction of the second Temple around the year 70 of the Christian era (known as the Second Temple period), the idea of both general and individual resurrection was firmly embedded in Jewish rabbinical thought. "What had been a rare exception in the early period became the basis for a general expectation in the late one . . . the previous exception becomes the norm."[6] Although there were differences of opinion regarding the resurrected life beyond death—for example, the Sadducees expected no such thing—the doctrine of the resurrection of the dead became central during this time of the Second Temple.

Of course the tension remained (and remains to this day) between God's promises of life and the grim reality of death—since both death and life appear to be God's own doing. Madigan and Levenson conclude their historical tracing of resurrection thought in Hebrew Scripture and later rabbinical writing in this way:

> Although bad things do indeed happen to good people, they are not the last word. The last word, rather, is a good thing—in this case God's miraculous intervention into history to grant the dead of all generations new life as he finally secures his triumph over evil and suffering and establishes on earth the kingdom over which he already reigns in the higher realm.
>
> In this view of things, death does not lose its reality or its grimness but only its finality . . . In this way, death must be seen as an opponent of the living God whose faithfulness to his promises will not be self-evident until death is vanquished and eliminated . . . Death, no less than life, is part of God's plan, but it is—or can be made into—only one stage of the plan, and not the last. The gracious king who gives and withdraws life will give it again.[7]

And in the meantime where are the dead? This is the question that haunted rabbinic and early Christian thought, and that still haunts us today. Where is Mary's mother? My mom and

6. Ibid., 165.

7. Ibid., 203.

dad? My husband? For the Second Temple writers, for many contemporary Jewish and Christian theologians, and perhaps from our own vantage point, the dead are "asleep," awaiting that final resurrection. However, from the point of view of those already dead, the weight of Scripture suggests that judgment and reward or punishment is meted out at the time of death. So we still speculate and often disagree with one another about such last things. But Scripture does supply hints, and perhaps that's the best we can go on in the life of faith.

To reiterate: deeply embedded in both Jewish and early Christian belief is the notion of a person as embodied and not complete until resurrected and made new in God's transformed creation. But from this historical period onward, this holistic idea of human being was (and is) in tension with a dualistic conception of humans as somehow body and soul, or body *versus* soul. Some major currents of Greco-Roman philosophy during this Second Temple period and after heavily influenced both rabbinical and early Christian ideas of resurrection, placing emphasis on the immortality of the soul apart from bodily matter.

So it was the case that in Second Temple Jewish thought controversies swirled regarding the nature of human being—holistic versus dualistic. Such controversies pitted Hebraic, holistic thought against Hellenistic inspired Judaism. The latter espoused Platonic notions of evil matter versus divinely sparked soul. And such tensions carried over into Christianity from its earliest days.

Thus, Jesus was born into a world (this same time of the Second Temple) that for the most part hoped for bodily resurrection and vindication of God's righteous covenant people and a re-creation of all the natural world—while expecting everlasting perdition for those who had strayed. But to stress again, resurrection was not a universal expectation. Some Jews eschewed the idea of resurrection entirely, and others—under the influence of Greek thought—held other, entirely spiritual ideas of eternal life.

Jesus, himself, clearly was heir to the first strand of belief—that the godly righteous, including the repentant, would be resurrected at the end time, while unrepentant sinners would suffer everlasting punishment both after death and in the end. As an example of Jesus' belief in this regard, Madigan and Levenson point out his appeal to the Hebrew patriarchs—Abraham, Isaac, and Jacob—in affirming the resurrection of the dead in his controversy with the Sadducees (Matt 22:31–32; Mark 12:26–27; Luke 20:37–38). They conclude that "Jesus had close affinities with the Pharisaic Jewish sect, which emphatically endorsed the doctrine of resurrection, as did the rabbis after them."[8]

But what Jesus's followers were not prepared for was his assertion that he, himself, would rise from the dead after "three days." Perhaps to put it mildly, no one among his followers or his people expected that a single individual—apart from the peoples or the whole nation at the end time—would rise as the "first fruit" and harbinger of the transformed and redeemed world to come. There simply was no place for them to fit such a notion into their imaginations, into their expectations of such a reality. They were puzzled. The idea seemed bizarre—and shocking—then, as well as now.

Which brings me to the empty tomb. On the whole, and despite some different strands of thought as we have seen, the Jews' expectation for resurrection during the time of Jesus (in the first century of the common era) had to do with bodies, "with creation in its concrete corporeality, not with immaterial spirits." For those at the time who believed that God would raise the dead at the end of time, "there is not evidence that resurrection [belief] in the first century . . . could have meant something non-bodily."[9]

Few deny the historical fact that Jesus died on a Roman cross and that the tomb where his body was buried came up empty on the third day. But in his book, *Resurrection: A Christian Theology of Presence and Absence*, Brian Robinette (whom we have just quoted)

8. Ibid., 211.

9. Robinette, *Grammars of Resurrection*, 118.

insists that you can't leap from the fact of the empty tomb to the assertion of Jesus' bodily resurrection on that first Easter morning. In order to get from there to here you have to make a leap of faith, that leap founded in large part on the testimony of St. Paul and the gospel writers. Despite a pervasive dualism absorbed from Greek and Roman philosophical thought at the time, the belief in Jesus's singular resurrection from the grave affirmed God's final embrace of time and matter. Such belief also affirmed an understanding of human being as finally incomplete until body and soul are again united in the end. As Robinette insists, our integrity as human beings rests on God's power to save us as we are made.

And he sees a certain reasonableness to this assertion. Although early Christian writers (as well as our sibling Jewish kin) had different and nuanced views on the subject, you can see a certain pattern in their thought. Robinette says that they figured that "because God originally fashioned human beings as a composite of body and soul, the fulfillment of the whole person logically required fulfillment of the body."[10]

The writings of St. Paul figure into the heart of this discussion. If we can consider Paul the earliest gospel writer, much has been made of his distinction between "bodily" flesh and "spiritual" flesh. Claims have been made based on this distinction between flesh and spirit to argue that Paul rejected as sinful and unworthy of redemption this body we are born into. Since we are arguing the opposite, it might be worthwhile to linger a bit on what Paul meant in this regard, and consider how his idea of spiritual body

---

10. Ibid., 123. But as Robinette also points out, if you don't accept the proposition that the body is an essential and integrated aspect of human being, then you won't buy the reasonableness and necessity of embodiment in the end time as endorsed by Irenaeus and other early Christian writers. But as I have argued throughout this present work—drawing from secular fields as diverse as evolutionary neuroscience, psychology, and anthropology—in addition to such theological arguments—there are strong and even empirically based reasons to embrace such a holistic understanding of human nature.

relates to our understanding of Jesus' resurrected body as depicted in the gospels.

In 1 Corinthians 15, Paul gives his answer when someone asks, "how are the dead raised? With what kind of body do they come?" Paul responds in vv. 42–44 thus: "What is sown is perishable, what is raised is imperishable. It is sown in dishonor, it is raised in glory. It is sown in weakness, it is raised in power. It is sown a physical body, it is raised a spiritual body." It is easy to see how some could interpret this passage as Paul rejecting the material body in favor of a resurrected but spiritual life in the end. But let's look more closely, trying to understand Paul's use of language and the contextual meaning of his words.

Both Joel Green[11] and Brian Robinette make the same argument. First, Paul's use of a seed metaphor for resurrected life suggests that there is continuity between what dies and what comes to resurrected life. And for the Jews of Paul's day and culture, human being—dead or alive—meant an embodied, whole person. It turns out that the contrast Paul is making here is between a human being in a natural state (weak, frail, sinful, and corruptible—uninhabited and unenlivened by God's Spirit, giving life) and a human being in a transformed state (incorruptible, purified, and redeemed—transfigured and transformed by God's power, God's Spirit).

At the end of this passage, Paul becomes beautifully lyrical as he writes

> Listen, I will tell you a mystery! We will not all die, but we will all be changed, in a moment, in the twinkling of an eye, at the last trumpet. For the trumpet will sound, and the dead will be raised imperishable, and we will be changed. For this perishable body must put on imperishability, and this mortal body must put on immortality. When this perishable body puts on imperishability, and this mortal body puts on immortality, then the saying that is written will be fulfilled. "Death has been swallowed up in victory." "Where, O death, is your victory? Where O death is your sting?"

11. Green, *Body, Soul, and Human Life.*

Robinette concludes that the difference between the fleshly body and the spiritual body is a question of what animates a human being. The former natural body is enlivened by its own human power, motivated and driven by its everyday finiteness toward limited, sinful ends. In contrast, the spiritual body is that same human body, but now empowered by God's grace-filled spirit. The risen and transformed body is the same human person, now vitalized by the influence of God's spiritual power, becoming "a new somatic reality." "The same identifiable, recognizable, and accountable identity . . . is transfigured into a *radically different form*, but remains this *created being in its wholeness*."[12]

If such continuity of our physical bodies from life through death into God's final re-creation is true, then as I have maintained here and will emphasize in the next section to this chapter—what we do with our bodies in this life is profoundly important. As Robinette states clearly throughout his work, "I will be my body" in the end. "*What we do with our bodies matters quite precisely because it is our bodies that will be raised.*"[13]

Such an understanding of transformed physical reality at resurrection also perhaps makes clearer our understanding of Jesus's resurrected flesh in the gospels' portrayals of his post-Easter appearances. He appears in fleshly form (for example, eating once again with his disciples, inviting Thomas to touch his wounded side), but his body is now animated by a godly power that allows him to pass through locked doors, to appear suddenly and disappear at will, having an altered physical appearance which is on occasion not recognized by others.

Such a transformed, resurrected body has been characterized by the authors I have cited here as "transphysical." Such a notion is by no means an attempt to explain in any causal way such a mystery beyond our comprehension. The term merely "puts a label on

---

12. Thiselton, *The First Epistle to the Corinthians*, quoted in Robinette, *Grammars of Resurection*, 157 (italics original).

13. Robinette, *Grammars of Resurrection*, 156 (italics original).

the demonstrable fact that the early Christians envisaged a body which was still robustly physical but also significantly different from the present. If anything . . . we might say not that it will not be *less* physical, as though it were some kind of ghost or apparition, but more."[14]

But Jesus didn't just appear in such a transfigured or trans-physical state in order to confirm God's power over death itself, or to affirm God's promise fulfilled in him as a "firstfruit" or harbinger of a general resurrection for all. No, he also launched his followers' mission into the world to begin to fulfill his first public statement: that the kingdom of God *is* at hand. Paul says in Romans, "If the Spirit of him who raised Jesus from the dead dwells in you, he who raised Christ from the dead will give life to your mortal bodies also through his Spirit that dwells in you" (Rom 8:11). The asser-tion of Jesus's bodily resurrection and belief based on testimony of his postresurrection appearances recorded in the New Testament Scriptures "launched a claim on the world," as N. T. Wright put it. Because God's spirit now dwells within material reality saved by God's power, "we are emboldened to say that the future is breaking in upon the present, vivifying and fermenting creation in a pro-gression toward that day when we will experience the full redemp-tion of our bodies."[15]

Now to my ears this idea of God's future even now breaking in echoes some of Teilhard's thought. God now presses in upon us, calling us and enabling us by his grace to create ourselves and the world around us anew. God is "at the tip of my pen, my spade, my brush" We are called to fashion our ensouled selves, evolve and flourish through the works which challenge us, as well as through the losses we contend with as we live out our days.

But between Paul and Teilhard and to this day in the twenty-first century, Western thought concerning human nature and the possibility of resurrected, bodily life has continued to develop and

14. Wright, *The Resurrection of the Son of God*, 477–78.
15. Robinette, *Grammars of Resurrection*, 153.

has taken some very interesting turns. And I think it's important briefly to consider this history, before launching into our discussion of flourishing now in anticipation of Kingdom flourishing at the end of time.

After Paul's writings, hints of doubt concerning bodily resurrection appear already in the Gospel of John in the figure of "doubting Thomas." Following that last gospel's writing and reflecting continued controversy concerning human nature and what was essential to being human, the extrabiblical *Gospel of Thomas* was apparently written by a member of the Thomas community—part of a docetic movement in the early church (*docetic*, which means "to seem" or "to appear" only). Those espousing such docetic beliefs assumed that Jesus only seemed to die, that his flesh was not real but only a phantasm. Thus, flesh itself was not essential to what was really real, namely the soul or spirit, and so on. In short, matter and spirit do not need to co-exist.

Such dualistic understandings of human being and the afterlife have played a role in the history of thought, both in early rabbinic controversies as well as down through the Middle Ages and beyond in Christian and Judaic tradition. To risk oversimplifying by skipping the details, we can say that with the rise of rationalism and empiricism during the seventeenth-century Enlightenment, the split between body and soul (or mind) became more explicit—at least in learned circles.[16]

The knowing subject observed and measured the world of material objects, and the self became identified with the workings of the rational mind. In the process, "heaven" became a spiritualized place where souls went after death and the body as material object became separated off from this spiritual realm. Because Jesus's bodily resurrection remained foundational to Christian thought (thus, the resurrected body remained hard to ignore), a final bodily resurrection at the end time remained part of orthodox

16. For an extended and very readable discussion of this history see Wright, *Surprised by Hope*.

thinking during this period. But in the meantime, and before the end of it all in God's re-creation, body and soul became quite distinct entities in both life and after death.

This modern worldview extending from about the time of the seventeenth-century Enlightenment and into the twentieth century has—in many intellectual quarters—given way to what is referred to as the postmodern era. That is, the methods and products of modernism, with its practitioners' faith in empirical ways of measuring, testing, and thus knowing reality have increasingly been questioned by philosophers, scientists, theologians, and other writers. Faith in our rational power undergirding dogmatic certainty in both science and theology has become increasingly undermined.

Since we are only concerned here with the question of resurrection belief and the understanding of human embodiment in our contemporary period, I will again risk oversimplifying by tracing out what I think is significant for our purposes here. In general terms, the spirit of this age is to recognize the limits of human reason, accepting the fact that all knowledge is context bound. So generally speaking, dogmatic assertions are suspect, and rational thought is considered only one route of several to reach for truth (albeit only partial and limited and again, context bound). Other routes of knowing include the whole field of aesthetics: Drama, fiction, poetry, visual art, dance, and ritual.

Thus both science and art are now embraced by many as viable methods of knowing. And at least in some quarters, each domain coexists as respectable partners in uncovering some sense of reality—as meaningful truth for our lives as human beings in a shared world. We have moved from imagining that we could embrace absolute truths in any domain to the search for some human truths that can be gleaned by various means.

But the interesting thing here, and it has direct bearing on the notion of resurrected embodiment, is this: as science has become more modest in its universal claims, the domains of science that have had a major impact on our understanding of embodiment and human nature are the disciplines of cognitive and evolutionary psychology, as well as evolutionary neuroscience. These are the very disciplines that I have drawn from here, contributing to the foundations of this project.

In short, these brain sciences assume a model of human being as an embodied mind—a "thinking piece of meat" as someone has put it. Scientists working in these fields view human beings as an amalgam of body- and brain-based mind, an integrated body/mind at the level of conscious, intentional experience, and at the level of habitual behaviors and automatic biological processes that keep us going over the course of a lifetime. *But for the most part, out of this scientific base, the question of embodiment or of the embodied person in any afterlife—re-created, redeemed, or not—has been eliminated.* That is, *most* of the scientific thinkers in these fields have pretty much eliminated the notion of soul and certainly the mystery of God from the equation. One of the leading lights of the new thinking in philosophy, Mark Johnson, concluded that "the person you are cannot survive the death of your body."[17]

In the middle of this philosophical and scientific mix, there are thinkers of the middle way, writers who intentionally remain agnostic as to questions of an afterlife and the role of God and God's promises regarding resurrected life in our personal or final endings. For example, in his book titled *Perfection*,[18] Michael Hyde suggests somewhat ambiguously that God may in fact call humans to an evolving and more perfected state. But Hyde chooses to focus on the plane of human endeavor and the science of biotechnology (for example, gene therapy for the purpose of possible specific disease eradication) as primary contributor to our longings for perfection. With science's methods, of course, God cannot be "proved" in any case.

17. Johnson, *The Meaning of the Body*, 280.
18. Hyde, *Perfection*.

Still there are other contemporary science voices who take a bolder approach, several of which I have drawn upon in earlier chapters. Nancey Murphy's *Bodies and Souls or Spirited Bodies?*, Francis Collins's *The Language of God*, Joel Green's *What about the Soul?*, and Andrew Newberg and Mark Waldman's *How God Changes Your Brain*,[19] are cases in point. While recognizing the limits of the scientific enterprise, their own faith stances shape their larger worldviews to include God's probable workings in our world and in our end. The refusal to equate self with just the soul— the incomprehensibility of my self without my body—undergirds our sense of the sacredness of human life and fuels the contemporary debates regarding abortion and end-of-life medical decisions.

Finally, as Joel Green and others haves stressed, the possibility of bodily resurrection does lie outside and beyond our power as human beings. In that sense, Mark Johnson is right. The belief in final resurrection is just that, a belief resting on faith alone in God's power to keep God's promise of life to his creatures in the end. Resurrection is only possible as a gracious act of God. And this hope, this belief, has never disappeared from our human longing. As Caroline Walker Bynum concludes in her detailed history of Christian resurrection theology, even in the height of controversy, and despite persistent tension arising from dualistic strands of thought, our hope in the resurrected life and final flourishing in a new and redeemed creation persists to this day.

THE FLOURISHING LIFE NOW:
DANCING BEFORE THE FACE OF GOD

As Teilhard says, "God is at the tip of my pen," God's kingdom grace is manifest in the world about us, the kingdom of God has come near, and is even now, from time to time, shining through

---

19. Murphy, *Bodies and Souls or Spirited Bodies?*; Collins, *The Language of God*; Green, *What about the Soul?*; Newberg and Waldman, *How God Changes Your Brain*. In all fairness, I should point out that Mark Waldman is agnostic on the question of God, but Newberg is much less so.

our dark days. Yes, God's kingdom is visible in glimpses now and then as Jesus demonstrated. But you and I need "open eyes" even to begin to see these glimpses.

The journalist Sara Miles (whom we met in chapter 2) describes such glimpses in her autobiographical accounts published over the last few years. Here's a little scene borrowed from her new work, *Jesus Freak*. In it she continues her story (begun in her *Take This Bread*) as lay minister in St. Gregory's Episcopal Church in San Francisco—a congregation accustomed to experimental forms of liturgical worship.[20] If you remember, after a lifetime of agnosticism and just plain nonbelief, Sara had had a profound conversion experience at St. Gregory's after she wandered in one day and, out of curiosity, participated in a Eucharistic service. She stayed, and that church became the center of Sara's life.

As I described earlier, Sara singlehandedly convinced St. Gregory's to start a weekly soup program—not as an evangelistic tool but as a service to all the needy who came . . . service period (as she likes to put it). And out of that early experience, the mission expanded into their neighborhood—involving restaurants and chefs who banded together and offered free dining to all comers one night a week. And after one of these nights—held at a dive of a Chinese place—where they'd served 250 meals to the needy, as well as to those who just wanted to hang out and be part of the party, Sara and a few others from St. Gregory's decided to end the night (around midnight by the time they'd begun to clean up) with a Eucharist right there in that restaurant.

Now the hostess had warned that it wasn't going to work— that after a shift the cooks and waiters just wanted to go home or go to a bar and relax. But as it turns out, most everybody stayed— the cooks and waiters and hostess and dishwasher—those who never set foot in any church, the unchurched and the unbelievers . . . along with some curious few guests who had also stayed to watch. Sara says, "We celebrated Eucharist at midnight in the

20. Miles, *Jesus Freak*; Miles, *Take This Bread*.

middle of [that shabby] room, lit by strings of Christmas lights glinting off the metallic horse posters. My feet hurt more than they had in twenty years, and my shirt was slippery with grease. The waiters and dishwasher came out, curious, as I handed Paul a loaf of French bread.

> "He held it up, saying the ancient Hebrew prayer. 'Blessed be God, ruler of the universe, who brings forth grain from the earth,' he chanted.
>
> "'Now we share the bread with each other,' Paul instructed . . . 'It's Jesus' table, so the bread is for everybody.'"
>
> [Then Sara said, quoting Isaiah,] "Come all who are hungry . . . come and eat, without money, without price. The Lord has made a promise to love you faithfully forever: You shall go out with joy, and be led forth with peace."
>
> 'Amen!' Paul said."[21]

"Amen," others around them whispered. And they shared with each other.

Well, it turned out that not only did the Chinese owner give all the proceeds to St. Gregory's soup kitchen, but those unchurched waiters and waitresses walked over and handed Sara their evening's donations, and another waiter slipped her forty more bucks for the cause.

Sara said, "That's it . . . That's communion." And finally one of the waitresses murmured "Wow, that was wild . . . Everyone was like, oh, ritual. Like we needed it but didn't know what it was." She said, "It's really different to end the night thinking we made something together."[22]

And what they made together . . . was kingdom come.

Our flourishing is always flourishing-in-community. As Sara Miles so vividly describes, our own human flourishing always involves

21. Miles, *Jesus Freak*, 54–56.
22. Ibid., 56.

extending that flourishing to others in one way or another. And this idea of growth in kingdom life now has its roots deep in our Judeo-Christian history and culture.

Early on in this chapter and drawing from Madigan and Levinson's work, I said that Jews and Christians have grown up as siblings. And since the early Christian era, both rabbinical scholars and the early Christian church fathers fought the same battle against those who doubted the final resurrection of the embodied person. For both streams of orthodox thought, the whole person would be redeemed and justified and liberated in a new creation. And for both streams of thought, living that redeemed life begins *now* in the life of Torah and in the life of discipleship. For the devout Jew, life without Torah wisdom represents a kind of death. Only turning toward wise choices enjoined by Torah practice leads to repentance and righteous life. Obedience to the law (e.g., observing the Sabbath, doing good deeds, feeding the poor) gives a foretaste of the world to come. For faithful Jews, that final, resurrected victory requires both the power of God and the righteous living of the faithful. Final flourishing requires both.

For the Christian, N. T. Wright describes the essential connection between Jesus's death and resurrection and the inauguration of his kingdom ministry—proclaiming justice and mercy and forgiveness of sin in the life of the redeemed, and the restoration of God's reign in the world even now. His words are worth repeating here.

> When we reintegrate what should never have been separated—the kingdom-inaugurating public work of Jesus and his redemptive death and resurrection—we find that the gospels tell a different story . . . It is the story of God's kingdom being launched on earth as in heaven, generating a new state of affairs in which the power of evil has been decisively defeated, the new creation has been decisively launched, and Jesus' followers have been commissioned and equipped to put that victory and that inaugurated new world into practice. Atonement, redemption, and salvation are what happen on

the way because engaging in this work demands that people themselves be rescued from the powers that enslave the world in order that they can in turn be rescuers. To put it another way, if you want to help inaugurate God's kingdom, you must follow in the way of the cross, and if you want to benefit from Jesus's saving death, you must become part of his kingdom project . . . a salvation that is both *for* humans and, *through* saved humans, for the wider world.[23]

Wright takes pains to insist that living the eschatological or kingdom life now is not a Pollyannaish view of blissful living. No, the following of this way is in many cases hard and God's kingdom is built in a fallen world full of suffering and injustice. But as he points out, our future hope for a resurrected and flourishing life won by Jesus' victory over death is the firm basis for our hope in the present, suffering world we live in. Our now imperfect matter *does* matter. For we will be our redeemed bodies in the end.

Wright says that "heaven and earth . . . are made for each other, and at certain points they intersect and interlock." And it is the risen Jesus who is the ultimate point of that intersection— the risen Christ who is with us now in His transformed and spiritualized body within that Godly plane which intersects our own daily lives. And we are called to join our creative lives with God's own purpose, to become points of intersection in union with Him—in order to further God's kingdom in this world which is even now being made new.

Pierre Teilhard de Chardin reminds us that we evolve over time—that our lives, our very selves, are fashioned over our lifetimes by what we do and by what we deal with, by the activities we engage in and by what happens to us along the way and in the end. And God presses in upon us through both our choices and in those losses and sufferings which we do not choose, but which we both experience and withstand. We are called to flourish in the living of the lives that we are given. And in the process of

23. Wright, *Surprised by Hope*, 204–5.

that personal flourishing in communion with one another, we are called to extend God's coming kingdom even now.

So to voice the question that I asked at the beginning of this work, how can we live this flourishing life in anticipation of our final flourishing in the end time? What can you and I do to help bring in the kingdom, to live as flourishing and as creative a self as possible in this meantime, to spread God's beauty and justice and peace in union with God's purpose?

To answer these questions, I want to come back full circle, returning to our discussion of the Emerging Church phenomenon in this country and abroad. As I have stressed throughout this book, we are social creatures, engaged with and interconnected with one another, creating our meaning out of the community we share and shaping our brains in the dynamic living of our lives. Basic and foundational to this fact are two sound psychological principles described earlier: 1) what you do is what you become; and 2) community shapes your embodied self—what you do, what you see, and what you make of it.

With respect to the *first* behavioral principle, if you hang out with bad folks and do bad things, you gradually become a bad person. In contrast, if you join yourself to others who lead godly lives, if you emulate and mimic their behavior, if you shape your behavior after saintly models, you become a better person along the way. And leaders in the Emerging Church movement say, "try it on, try it out. See how it fits." And in the trying on, you become something new.

With respect to the *second* behavioral principle, community shapes individual lives. In fact, the practices you learn in community do shape you at the most basic, embodied level. Such practices—prayer, meditation, ritual, singing, drama, dancing, serving others—shape your very brain and thus shape your conscious attention to the world about you. A corollary to this is what's referred to as "group amplification." Group power amplifies the behavior of individuals embedded in that group. If you join a radical movement, your radical tendencies will become more so, will amplify over time. If you join a life-affirming movement, your growth tendencies will be group amplified. (Such is the principle at the base of successful twelve-step Alcoholics Anonymous programs.)

Both of these principles are essential in understanding the success of all communities which engage in kingdom building activities. Such open, welcoming, and spirited places of worship and service bring life to the communities around them and enhance the flourishing of those who join with them in furthering God's purposes in this world.

I am broadening the circle of emerging churches to include any church community that conforms to a certain open pattern of worship, belief, and practice—whether it sees itself as part of the Emerging Church movement or not. These are communities that embrace orthodox and ancient beliefs and traditions without rigidly clinging to dogmatic claims to absolute knowledge. And they also are worship communities which are welcoming places, open to new practices of aesthetic expression in worship, as well as fresh and contemporary forms of liturgy and ritual. Such communities can be launching places for kingdom work enabling those who join themselves to God's work to bridge from worship to the world beyond their doors.

In writing about the kingdom of God, Frederick Buechner once wrote that although it's God and God's power that bring about that kingdom, "we can drive back the darkness a little" and "make green places among ourselves."[24] So how do we drive back that darkness . . . even a little?

There are voices from the Emerging Church movement that answer this question by stressing spiritual formation that goes beyond individual practice to communal action. In this regard, Doug Pagitt refers to various categories of spirituality in the formation of our embodied souls. He speaks of a *spirituality of physicality* in terms of the way we lead our whole lives, Sunday through

24. Buechner, *Secrets in the Dark*, 118.

Saturday, week in and week out, being Christian in and with our total selves. He describes a *spirituality of hospitality* as not limited to coffee hours after church but expanding out to others who walk in the door, no matter how different; a hospitality that includes a connectedness to those who live in our neighborhood and beyond—who share a common bond of humankindness with us.

Pagitt describes a *spirituality of dialogue* in reading Scripture and works of theology, an openness to the Spirit's movement among us as we create new insights through conversation. He sees a *spirituality of creativity* as an invitation to engage with God's work as co-creators building the good and the beautiful in this world—a better creation that God will bless and transform in God's kingdom come. And for him a *spirituality of service* seeks to share God's blessing to all in the form of mercy, justice, and love beyond the writing of a mission statement. Pagitt's categories of spirituality make clear the holistic and all-embracing nature of these emerging, twenty-first-century communities.

In her *Let the Bones Dance*,[25] Marcia Shoop says that God's spirit is "entangled in us, in the pulsing of our blood, in the beating of our hearts, in the horizons of our imaginations."[26] Like Teilhard and others whom I've drawn from here, Shoop sees human life as in many ways *tragic* ("with loss written in our bodies in permanent ink"), *relational* (inherently communal as we engage with others and the world at large), and *ambiguous* (with our grasp of reality always culturally bound, finite, and subject to flux and uncertainty).

These hallmarks of human being echo themes I have attempted to develop across the chapters in this work, and are coherent with the spiritual categories given by Pagitt. These spiritual aspects of emerging and open church communities resonate deeply with what makes us human and our whole selves (remember the elephant and its rider?) can be shaped positively and enhanced in

25. Shoop, *Let the Bones Dance*.
26. Ibid., 125.

such communal engagement. What you do is what you become; community shapes your whole self.

Beyond individual practices that shape our brain and color our consciousness of the world about us, there are communal practices that are life enhancing and lend themselves to a flourishing coherence at all levels of human experience. Shoop indicates three practices linked to our tragic, communal, and ambiguous lives.

First, we humans are in many ways pathetic and flawed, and we grow weak and we die in the end. But Shoop says we can reach deep down into that self-knowledge and express compassion for others who also suffer. We can confess the truth of our lives by being honest about our flaws, and we can forgive one another for our common frailties. In my own life, once I confronted my own faulty self and the evil I was capable of, I found also a sense of compassion for others who sin. I discovered a self no longer willing to cast the first stone—a more compassionate self in the process. Honesty, compassion, and forgiveness are linked healing practices that can transform our suffering selves in the meantime of our lives.

Second, we are interdependent with one another, we are relational and communal beings, we are all in this together. And with a keen recognition of such common bonding, we share our communal meal with each other as a foretaste of that final, eschatological banquet at the end time. As Shoop puts it, this ritual re-members and celebrates Jesus's life now among us "to guide us, to in-form us, to dwell in us, and to transform us." Like the rest of the embodied sacraments such as baptism and anointing, its truth lies beyond and beneath words, expressing and embodying its core meaning in the ritual acts of feeding and nourishing one another.

Third, the ambiguity of our human condition also allows for creativity, discovery, and adventure. For Shoop, such ambiguity is perhaps expressed uniquely well in the songs we sing and the dances we dance . . . in the music that resonates with our very fibers. We have inherited from our ancient ancestors the capacity for rhythm, music, and dance. Because language is so dominant in our western culture as the preferred form of communication, this inborn capacity lies fallow for the most part, maybe even "lost" as a holistic, embodied language of its own, except at clubs, rock concerts, and in some church gatherings.

In fact, the only universal context for musical expression is a religious one. If you look throughout the world you will find music of some form as part of worship ceremonies. This is so because religions deal with the "irrational, spiritual, unseen reality of God." As a result, music, along with other rhythmic expressions such as dance, ritual, and sacrament, becomes the main means of grasping for, worshiping, and communicating with the Divine. As someone said, "If I could have said it, I wouldn't have needed to dance it!" Shoop sees churches that embrace various forms of music beyond standard hymnody as feeding our capacity for joyful exuberance and improvisation. Communities willing to experience not just piano and organ, but also drum, tambourine, and guitar, are vital places of worship. Those that welcome many forms of musical expression—from Bach to jazz, from Taize to gospel—nourish our embodied souls. In contrast, other (often mainline) churches which stifle such expression have increasingly empty pews as especially their younger members seek nourishment elsewhere.

Finally, a word about service: we began this section with a spotlight on Sara Miles's church, St. Gregory's in San Francisco, and considered the extraordinary soup kitchen she runs out of that place. Miles insists that there's no intentional evangelistic purpose in their hand extended to those who are in need. It's just service, period! Out of the largesse that God has blessed them with, they give back to others. Of course there are other churches that we could point to in this regard. There's Church of the Holy Apostles in Chelsea, New York, and churches right here in Richmond, Virginia that do fantastic service to the needy in this way.

Pagitt's spirituality of service is an attitude of openness to neighbors, a welcoming embrace to those in the neighborhood, an open door to those in need simply as fellow humans occupying the same boat for a while. This reaching out expresses a spirit of engagement with and caring about the world down the street and across the way. Wright also talks about bridging out of the church space into the larger community, working for better housing and better schools and more beautiful parks, to working for God's justice and beauty and mercy. This world can become better and flourish through God's kingdom grace and our creative effort.

IMAGES

An early eighteenth-century "black plantation preacher [writes] that 'the way in which we worship [is] almost indescribable. The singing [is] accompanied by a certain ecstasy of motion, clapping of hands, tossing of heads.'" And into the middle of this ring of black slaves, clapping and singing, move dancers one by one—shouting and whirling round and round in circles. And after some time in such ecstatic trances, only the strong and able-bodied stay in the ring, while the weak drop out to the surrounding circle to watch and clap. The men and women in the center of this body-in-motion toss their heads back to the rhythm of the chorus, beating out the time with hands and feet, "in the constant shuffle of the ring."[27]

In this way they praised the Lord and felt set free from their daily labors, celebrating the joy of being alive in the Spirit.

A homeless man, in tattered clothes, wearing goggles and carrying his life's possessions in two Safeway plastic bags, moves down the main aisle of a cathedral. Worshipers on that Sunday morning are singing a rousing gospel hymn ("Order my steps

27. Ehrenreich, *Dancing in the Street*, 216–17.

in your word, Dear Lord, Lead me, guide me, every day. Send your anointing, Father, I pray. Order my steps in your word . . ."), and the man moves on down the aisle to the front of the church, drops his bags by the pulpit, and with a beatific look on his face, begins to dance to the music. The people keep on singing . . . and he keeps on dancing. And on and on they go, verse after verse. And when the music finally stops, the homeless fellow lifts up high a receiver belonging to an old-fashioned, push-button phone, with wires dangling. And he shouts "I've got a call for you. God told me to come here."[28] Alleluia!

On most Sunday mornings in Richmond, a man stands on the corner of Main and 17th Street, and he dances . . . first dipping this way, then dipping that way, gracefully bowing to oncoming cars as he does his sidewalk dance—moving to music he alone hears in his head, smiling in some kind of ecstatic trance, waving to me as I pass him, connected by some unseen cord, joined by the Spirit, moved by the rhythm of his steps.

They filed into a bar in Sheffield, England, on Saturday night to celebrate Eucharist together, to pray, and yes, to dance. Not a "churchy" dance says the speaker, but a "normal" dance—like you'd see at a rave or a disco. They dance and they dance to the beat as they worship. And the boundaries between the individual dancers drop away as they meld into a communal group . . . bonded as one organism, moving, clapping, in and out and back and forth, worshiping God whose Spirit surrounds and permeates them . . . that Lord of the Dance who leads their improvised steps and fills their hearts with exuberance and joy.[29]

28. Shoop, *Let the Bones Dance*, 174.
29. Baker and Gay, *Alternative Worship*.

~

So tables aside! Any dance at all.
I'd loved our flight from the formal,
Our broken observance, Rock and roll.
The Twist, Disco, Sweet and manic,
Our blare of rapture. Alone. Freelance.

But I yearn again for ritual, organic
Patterns, circlings, the whorled dance . . .

Openness. Again and again to realign.
Another face and the moves must begin
Anew. And we unfold into our design.
I want to dance for ever. A veil
Shakes between now-ness and infinity.
Touch of hands. Communal and frail.
Our courtesies weave a fragile city.[30]

~

And finally one of the waitresses murmurs, "Wow, that was wild
. . . Everyone was like, oh, ritual. Like we needed it but didn't know
what it was." She said, "It's really different to end the night thinking, we made something together."[31]

And what they made together was a bit of God's kingdom—
humankind flourishing, singing and dancing before the face of
God.

> I saw the holy city, the new Jerusalem, coming down out of
> heaven from God, prepared as a bride adorned for her hus-
> band. And I heard a loud voice from the throne saying, "See,
> the home of God is among mortals. He will dwell with them;
> they will be his peoples, and God himself will be with them;

30. O'Siadhail, "Dances," in *Poems 1975–1995*, 227.

31. Miles, *Jesus Freak*, 56.

he will wipe every tear from their eyes. Death will be no more; mourning and crying and pain will be no more, for the first things have passed away." And the one who was seated on the throne said, "See, I am making all things new. (Rev 21:2–5.)

Amen. And so shall it be.

Appendix

Resources for Embodied Practices

Baker, Jonny, and Doug Gay, with Jenny Brown. *Alternative Worship: Resources from and for the Emerging Church.* Grand Rapids: Baker, 2003.

Bloom, Anthony. *Beginning to Pray.* New York: Paulist, 1970.

Bond, Fiona. *The Arts in Your Church: A Practical Guide.* Carlisle, UK: Piquant, 2001.

Bourgeault, Cynthia. *Centering Prayer and Inner Awakening.* Cambridge: Cowley, 2004.

DeLeon, Roy. *Praying with the Body: Bringing the Psalms to Life.* Brewster, MA: Paraclete, 2009.

Henke, Linda Witte, *Marking Time: Christian Rituals for All Our Days.* Harrisburg, PA: Morehouse, 2001.

Klein, Patricia, *Worship without Words: The Signs and Symbols of Our Faith.* Brewster, MA: Paraclete, 2000.

Johnston, William. *Christian Zen.* 3rd ed. New York: Fordham University Press, 1997.

———. *Silent Music: The Science of Meditation.* New York: Harper & Row, 1974.

Pagitt, Doug, and the Solomon's Porch Community. *Reimagining Spiritual Formation: A Week in the Life of an Experimental Church.* Grand Rapids: Zondervan, 2003.

Reininger, Gustave, editor. *The Diversity of Centering Prayer.* New York: Continuum, 1999.

Tedeschi, Richard G., and Lawrence G. Calhoun. *Trauma & Transformation: Growing in the Aftermath of Suffering.* Thousand Oaks, CA: Sage, 1995.

Bibliography

Baker, Jonny, and Doug Gay, with Jenny Brown. *Alternative Worship: Resources from and for the Emerging Church*. Grand Rapids: Baker, 2004.

Beauregard, Mario, and Denyse O'Leary. *The Spiritual Brain: A Neuroscientist's Case for the Existence of the Soul*. New York: HarperOne, 2007.

Begley, Sharon. *Train Your Mind, Change Your Brain: How a New Science Reveals Our Extraordinary Potential to Transform Ourselves*. New York: Ballentine 2007.

Bloom, Anthony. *Beginning to Pray*. Deus Books. New York: Paulist, 1970.

Bruner, Jerome. *Acts of Meaning*. The Jerusalem-Harvard Lectures. Cambridge: Harvard University Press, 1990.

Buechner, Frederick. *Secrets in the Dark: A Life in Sermons*. New York: HarperCollins, 2005.

Bynum, Caroline Walker. *The Resurrection of the Body in Western Christianity, 200–1336*. Lectures on the History of Religions, new ser. 15. New York: Columbia University Press, 1995.

Collins, Francis. *The Language of God: A Scientist Presents Evidence for Belief*. New York: Free Press, 2006.

Csikszentmihalyi, Mihaly, and Isabella Selega Csikszentmihalyi, editors. *A Life Worth Living: Contributions to Positive Psychology*. Series in Positive Psychology. Oxford: Oxford University Press, 2006.

Day, Dorothy. *The Long Loneliness: The Autobiography of Dorothy Day*. New York: Harper, 1952.

Eakin, Paul John. *How Our Lives Become Stories: Making Selves*. Ithaca: Cornell University Press, 1999.

Ehrenreich, Barbara. *Dancing in the Street*. New York: Metropolitan, 2006.

Elie, Paul. *The Life You Save May Be Your Own: An American Pilgrimage*. New York: Farrar, Straus & Giroux, 2003.

Bibliography

Emmons, Robert, and Michael McCullough, editors. *The Psychology of Gratitude.* Series in Affective Science. Oxford: Oxford University Press, 2004.

Feierman, Jay R. *The Biology of Religious Behavior: The Evolutionary Origins of Faith and Religion.* Santa Barbara: Praeger, 2009.

"Fifty of the Most Inspiring Authors in the World." *Poets & Writers,* January/February 2010, 44–58. Online: http://www.pw.com/.

Green, Joel B., editor. *What about the Soul?: Neuroscience and Christian Anthropology.* Nashville; Abingdon, 2004.

———. *Body, Soul, and Human Life: The Nature of Humanity in the Bible.* Studies in Theological Interpretation. Grand Rapids: Baker Academic, 2008.

Haidt, Jonathan. *The Happiness Hypothesis: Finding Modern Truth in Ancient Wisdom.* New York: Basic Books, 2006.

Hyde, Michael J. *Perfection: Coming to Terms with Being Human.* Waco, TX: Baylor University Press, 2010.

Jamison, Kay Redfield. *Exuberance: The Passion for Life.* New York: Vintage, 2004.

Johnson, Mark. *The Meaning of the Body: Aesthetics of Human Understanding.* Chicago: University of Chicago Press, 2007.

Jones, Tony. *The New Christians: Dispatches from the Emergent Frontier.* A Living Way. San Francisco: Jossey-Bass, 2008.

Karr, Mary. *Lit: A Memoir.* New York: HarperCollins, 2009.

Keyes, Corey L. M., and Jonathan Haidt, editors. *Flourishing: Positive Psychology and the Life Well Lived.* Washington, DC: American Psychological Association, 2007.

Levy, Sandra M. *Imagination and the Journey of Faith.* Grand Rapids: Eerdmans, 2008.

Madigan, Kevin J., and Jon D. Levenson. *Resurrection: The Power of God for Christians and Jews.* New Haven: Yale University Press, 2008.

Martin, James. *The Jesuit Guide to (Almost) Everything: A Spirituality for Real Life.* New York: HarperOne, 2010.

Maxwell, Elizabeth, and Susan Shapiro, editors. *Food for the Soul: Selections from the Holy Apostles Soup Kitchen Writers' Workshop.* New York: Church Publishing, 2004.

McAdams, Dan. *The Stories We Live By: Personal Myths and the Making of the Self.* New York: Guilford, 1993.

McAdams, Dan, et al. editors. *Identity and Story: Creating Self in Narrative.* Washington, DC: American Psychological Association, 2007.

Miles, Sara. *Take This Bread: A Radical Conversion.* New York: Ballantine, 2007.

————. *Jesus Freak: Feeding, Healing, Raising the Dead*. San Francisco: Jossey-Bass, 2010.

Mithen, Steven. *The Singing Neanderthals: The Origins of Music, Language, Mind, and Body*. Cambridge: Harvard University Press, 2006.

Murphy, Nancey. *Bodies and Souls or Spirited Bodies?* Current Issues in Theology. Cambridge: Cambridge University Press, 2006.

Myers, David G. *The American Paradox: Spiritual Hunger in an Age of Plenty*. New Haven: Yale University Press, 2000.

Newberg, Andrew E., and Mark Robert Waldman. *How God Changes Your Brain*. New York: Ballantine, 2009.

O'Siadhail, Michael. *Poems 1975–1995*. Newcastle: Bloodaxe, 1999.

Pagitt, Doug, and the Solomon's Porch Community. *Reimagining Spiritual Formation: A Week in the Life of an Experimental Church*. Grand Rapids: Zondervan, 2003.

Péguy, Charles. *God Speaks: Religious Poetry*. Translated by Julian Green. New York: Pantheon, 1962.

Polkinghorne, Donald E., *Narrative Knowing and the Human Sciences*. SUNY Series in Philosophy of the Social Sciences. Albany: SUNY Press, 1988.

Robinette, Brian. *Grammars of Resurrection: A Christian Theology of Presence and Absence*. New York: Crossroad, 2009.

Sheldon, Kennon M. *Optimal Human Being: An Integrated Multi-Level Perspective*. Mahwah, NJ: Erlbaum, 2004.

Shenk, Joshua. "What Makes Us Happy?" *The Atlantic*, June 2009, 36–53.

Shoop, Marcia. *Let the Bones Dance: Embodiment and the Body of Christ*. Louisville: Westminster John Knox, 2010.

Simmons, Philip. *Learning to Fall*. New York: Bantam Dell, 2003.

Tedeschi, Richard G., and Lawrence G. Calhoun. *Trauma & Transformation: Growing in the Aftermath of Suffering*. Thousand Oaks, CA: Sage, 1995.

Teilhard de Chardin, Pierre. *The Divine Milieu*. Rev. Harper Torchbook ed. New York: Harper, 1968.

————. *Let Me Explain*. Edited by Jean-Pierre Demoulin. New York: Harper & Row, 1966.

Updike, John. *Telephone Poles and Other Poems*. New York: Knopf, 1963.

Vaillant, George. *Spiritual Evolution: A Scientific Defense of Faith*. New York: Broadway, 2008.

Viorst, Judith. *Necessary Losses*. New York: Simon & Schuster, 1986.

Wolpe, David. *Making Loss Matter: Creating Meaning in Difficult Times*. New York: Riverhead, 1999.

Wright, N. T. *The Resurrection of the Son of God*. Christian Origins and Question of God 3. Minneapolis: Fortress, 2003.

———. *Surprised by Hope: Rethinking Heaven, the Resurrection, and the Purpose of the Church.* San Francisco: HarperOne, 2008.